NAMES OF THE HOLY SPIRIT

NAMES OF THE HOLY SPIRIT

RAY PRITCHARD

MOODY PRESS
CHICAGO

All Scripture quotations, unless indicated, are taken from the *Holy Bible: New International Version*®. NIV®. Copyright © 1973, 1978, 1984 International Bible Society. Used by permission of Zondervan Publishing House. All rights reserved.

Scripture quotations marked KJV are taken from the King James Version.

Scripture quotations marked LB are taken from the *Living Bible,* © 1971 by Tyndale House Publishers. All rights reserved. Used by permission.

The use of selected references from various versions of the Bible in this publication does not necessarily imply publisher endorsement of the versions in their entirety.

ISBN: 0-8024-6045-3

5 7 9 10 8 6 4

Printed in the United States of America

Dedicated to my three sons
Joshua, Mark, and Nicholas
With the prayer that they may grow up to be
Men of God
Filled with the Holy Spirit

ACKNOWLEDGEMENTS

Many thanks to Gary and Dawn Olson, who allowed me the use of their house while they traveled to Florida. Thanks also to my wife Marlene for her constant encouragement and wise insight. A special thanks to Greg Thornton of Moody Press, for his friendship and support.

INTRODUCTION

To many Christians, the Holy Spirit is a mystery. He is the "hidden" member of the Trinity. The Father we know; the Son we know; but what about the Holy Spirit? Few believers understand who He is, why He came, or what He does in the world today. Fewer still understand the vital role He plays in the Christian life.

I don't think I'm going overboard in saying that a proper knowledge of the Holy Spirit's ministry is absolutely essential to finding peace, joy, and victory as a Christian. Many believers live far below their potential because they have never discovered the Holy Spirit. They know nothing about His power, His indwelling, His anointing, His intercession, His gifts, and the fruit He longs to produce in them.

But living without the Holy Spirit is like trying to drive a car with an empty gas tank. While we may not understand all the secrets of internal combustion, if we don't understand the need for gas, the car isn't going to get out of the driveway.

God doesn't demand that we be able to explain the intricacies of pneumatology (the doctrine of the Holy Spirit) in order to enjoy His blessings. However, some basic knowledge is essential for releasing His power in our lives.

This book is written to provide some of that basic knowledge. This isn't a full-length doctrinal study of the Holy Spirit. Certain areas relating to the Spirit aren't touched at all. However, you will no doubt discover many things about the Holy Spirit you didn't know before, especially material relating to His ministry in the Old Testament.

Writing about the names of the Holy Spirit poses a fascinating challenge because there aren't many proper names for the Spirit. Instead, the writers of the Bible used a combination of descriptive titles ("Spirit of the Living God," "Promised Holy Spirit," "Spirit of the Sovereign Lord") and a wide variety of symbols relating to the Spirit ("Seal," "Deposit," "Dew," "Oil"). Taken together, these 87 names reveal an amazing amount of information about the Holy Spirit. The first name occurs in Genesis 1:2 and the last one in Revelation 19:10. Thus, the work of the Spirit spans the Bible—from the earliest moments of creation to the crowning events of world history.

In treating each name, I have briefly sketched the context in which it appears. Where appropriate, I have also mentioned related Scriptures for those who wish to dig deeper. Each section closes with a few sentences of application and a short prayer.

Although such a study might be arranged in many ways, it seemed best to keep the names in their basic biblical order. Thus, we will begin in Genesis, move through the historical books, the poetical books, the major and minor prophets, the

Gospels, the book of Acts, the epistles, ending with the book of Revelation. By studying the names of the Holy Spirit in canonical order, we will get a flavor of how the Holy Spirit worked in different periods of biblical history.

I have tried to give special attention to the work of the Holy Spirit in the Old Testament since that is an often-neglected field of study. You may be amazed—as I was—to discover how much the Old Testament says about the ministry of the Spirit.

In the index, you will find all the names listed in this volume in alphabetical order, along with the primary Scripture reference. As you read this book, you may find yourself intrigued by one particular name or group of names. If so, I encourage you to spend some time in your own Bible study.

Although this book is based on the NIV, I have occasionally used a name either from my own study or from another translation.

My prayer is that this book will lead you to a new appreciation of the Holy Spirit and ultimately to a new dependence on His power in your life.

THE SPIRIT ABOVE THE WATERS

Now the earth was formless and empty,
darkness was over the surface of the deep, and
the Spirit of God was hovering over the waters.
(Genesis 1:2)

"In the beginning God created." With these five majestic words, the Bible declares that God Himself stands alone before the creation of the universe. How does He create the world? What is His first step? Genesis 1:2 informs us that the Holy Spirit was "hovering" above the waters. The word "hovering" suggests a bird tenderly protecting her helpless children in the nest.

Although much is shrouded in mystery, we may be sure of this: God's Spirit was there in the beginning, taking the formless mass, moving through the darkness, filling the emptiness, preparing the way for God to speak the creative word and bring light into the world.

Think of it! The mighty Spirit of God hovers over all creation. Without the Spirit, nothing that is made will come into being. He is there in the beginning, He moves through the chaos and darkness, He protects the prenatal creation.

We may be encouraged that God's Holy Spirit still hovers over the darkness today. Though we may not see Him or feel Him or reach out and touch him, yet He is there. He still moves through the emptiness of life, preparing the way for God to bring us out of the darkness and into the light once again.

O Lord, as Your Spirit once hovered over the dark chaos of creation, help me to believe that in the darkness of my life You are still there, still watching, still protecting. Thank You that the light of Your presence will shine again in my life. Amen.

BREATH OF LIFE

And the Lord God formed the man from the dust of the ground and breathed into his nostrils the breath of life, and man became a living being. (Genesis 2:7)

The Hebrew word *ruah* can be translated "breath" or "spirit." The phrase "breath of life," therefore, refers to more than simply the air that Adam breathed. It is the animating life force that comes only from God's Spirit. By itself, the body is simply "the dust of the ground"—a collection of chemical elements bound together as water and protein. But life comes only from the inbreathing of God's Spirit.

All that we are and have we owe to God who has brought us to life by His Spirit. What a contrast to many who boast of their worldly achievements—money, fame, and power. But those things do not last forever. All of it returns to the dust eventually.

Life comes only from God—a fact true both on the physical and spiritual planes. Just as we owe our physical life to the Spirit of God, we also owe our spiritual life to Him as well. For without the "inbreathing" of God's Spirit in the work of regeneration, we could not be born again.

Thank You, Father, for giving me the breath of life. Thank You also for the gracious work of Your Spirit in breathing into me new life through Jesus Christ. Amen.

Then the Lord said, "My Spirit will not contend with man forever, for he is mortal; his days will be a hundred and twenty years." (Genesis 6:3)

Racing across the generations, we come to the evil days before the great Flood. Instead of getting better, mankind had gone steadily downward. From the beauty of Eden, man swam in the gutter of open sin. The mighty sons of God (perhaps human rulers indwelt by evil spirits) saw the daughters of men (women willing to give themselves to immorality). The result of this ungodly union was the "nephilim"—mighty heroes who were themselves "fallen ones" (the literal meaning of the Hebrew word). Though powerful and mighty and able to "fall upon" others, they were sinners doomed to death like all other men.

The world was ripe for judgment because God saw evil covering the earth like a dirty blanket. Every thought of man's heart was rotten and corrupt. But even in this desperate situation, God's Spirit was not absent. He was "striving" or "contending" with mankind. Because He is the Spirit of truth, He constantly strives with men to move them toward truth and righteousness.

But the warning is clear. God's Spirit will not strive with man forever. Those who refuse His voice will eventually face God's judgment. In the days of Noah, God withheld final judgment for 120 years, but the rains of judgment finally fell from heaven, and a mighty flood covered the entire earth. Only Noah and his family were saved.

No one knows when judgment will finally fall, but sooner or later those who reject God's mercy will face His wrath.

Spirit of God, give me listening ears to hear Your voice speaking to me. May I never take You for granted, but respond quickly to Your leading in my life. Amen.

THE SERVANT

So he said, "I am Abraham's servant."
(Genesis 24:34)

A quick scan of Genesis 24 reveals that the Holy
Spirit is mentioned nowhere. What we find instead is a delightful story of the aged Abraham
sending his servant five hundred miles to find a
bride for his son Isaac. Where is the Holy Spirit in
this story? Many Bible students see the servant as
a beautiful illustration of the Holy Spirit's work in
salvation. In a general sense, we know that Abraham's offering of his son Isaac on Mount Moriah
(Genesis 22), is a picture of the Father offering His
Son at the cross. A similar symbolism may be
seen in Genesis 24. Just as Abraham sought a
bride for Isaac, even so our Heavenly Father seeks
a bride for His Son, the Lord Jesus Christ (2 Corinthians 11:2; Ephesians 5:26–27). Furthermore, the
servant was sent on a particular mission—to find
a bride. He travels a great distance with but one
goal in mind—to find a bride for his master's son.
In the same way, the Holy Spirit moves across the
earth wooing and winning men and women for Jesus Christ. The servant says nothing on his own
behalf but takes every opportunity to speak well of
Isaac. Even so, the Holy Spirit speaks not of Himself but glorifies Christ (John 16:13). When the
servant found Rebekah, he gave her gifts just as
the Spirit gives gifts to those who are in the body
of Christ (1 Corinthians 12:11). Finally, the servant

personally accompanied Rebekah on the journey to meet Isaac. In the same way, the Holy Spirit draws us into a personal relationship with Jesus Christ.

Perhaps the very length of Genesis 24 (67 verses) shows us something of God's heart for sinners. It was not an easy thing for the servant to find a bride for Isaac. It entailed a long and dangerous journey into unfamiliar territory. But the servant would not be turned away. Neither will the Holy Spirit be turned aside from His holy calling to find a bride for the Son of God.

Thank You, Father, for sending Your Spirit into the world to draw me to the Savior. Amen.

THE SPIRIT OF GOD

So Pharaoh asked them, "Can we find anyone like this man, one in whom is the spirit of God?" (Genesis 41:38)

In this case, Pharaoh spoke beyond his own wisdom. As a pagan ruler, he could hardly be expected to know about the Holy Spirit. Yet he recognized something different in Joseph's life, a power that gave him the ability to correctly interpret dreams. Perhaps Pharaoh thought that Joseph was following one of the many gods worshiped by the nations surrounding Egypt. Or perhaps he did in fact know (because Joseph told him) that this was the work of the Spirit of God.

But Pharaoh saw something in Joseph that couldn't be explained through any natural means. It was partly the ability to interpret dreams and partly the wisdom of the man himself. Both came from the Spirit of God.

When the Holy Spirit moves in our lives, even unbelievers will know the difference. Just as Joseph was promoted to become the Prime Minister of Egypt, even so the Holy Spirit's presence in our lives will open doors for greater service to God and man.

Holy Spirit, fill me with Your power so that even those who don't know You may see the difference You make in my life. Amen.

So Samuel took the horn of oil and anointed him in the presence of his brothers, and from that day on the Spirit of the Lord came upon David in power. (1 Samuel 16:13)

Once the Lord rejected Saul as king, that meant a new ruler had to be found. But where should Samuel begin looking? The Lord directed him to go to "Jesse of Bethlehem," for the Lord had chosen one of his sons to be the next king. But which one would it be? One by one, Jesse had seven of his sons pass before Samuel. Each time the Lord told Samuel, "Not this one." Only one son was left, the youngest, a boy named David, but he was out tending the sheep. When David was brought before Samuel, the Lord said, "He is the one." Whereupon Samuel anointed David with oil, and the Spirit of the Lord came upon him in great power.

Oil is a familiar biblical symbol of the Holy Spirit. In the Old Testament, priests and kings were anointed with oil as a means of setting them apart for special service to God. Oil also was used as fuel for lamps and for cleansing and sanctifying. In the New Testament, Jesus sent out the Twelve to minister in His name. They cast out demons and anointed sick people with oil (Mark 6:7–13). In James 5:14 we find instructions regarding elders anointing the sick with oil.

Just as the priests and kings must first be anointed with oil before service can begin, so the power of the Holy Spirit is necessary for all effective service for God. Just as oil is necessary for the lamp to give off light, so it is the Holy Spirit who gives us power to shine as the light of the world. Just as oil sanctifies priests and lepers, so the Holy Spirit sanctifies the children of God. Anointing the sick with oil reminds both the sick and the well that all true healing rests in God's hands alone.

Psalm 133 compares the oil running down Aaron's beard with the blessing of unity among the people of God. The oil of the Holy Spirit lubricates the body of Christ, bringing together Christians who would otherwise be separated from one another.

Psalm 45:7 mentions the "oil of joy," while Psalm 104:15 speaks of oil that makes the face shine. In Psalm 23:5, David praises God who anointed his head with oil. These passages typify the ministry of the Holy Spirit in bringing joy to the heart of the believer.

Father, Thank You for the oil of the Holy Spirit. May the "good oil" of the Spirit flow through me today. Amen.

THE DOUBLE PORTION

*"Let me inherit a double portion of your spirit,"
Elisha replied.* (2 Kings 2:9)

The spirit of Elijah is resting on Elisha.
(2 Kings 2:15)

Why did Elisha ask for a "double portion" of Elijah's spirit? The answer lies in the inheritance laws of the Old Testament. According to Deuteronomy 21:17, the firstborn son was entitled to a "double share" of the father's possessions. Although Elisha was not literally Elijah's son, he was truly his "firstborn" heir in terms of spiritual power.

Elisha was thus asking for a "double share" of the spiritual power Elijah possessed, power which came directly from the Holy Spirit at work in his life. He was not asking for material possessions, nor for a ministry twice as great as Elijah or the power to work twice as many miracles. All those things were secondary to the basic request: "May I receive a double portion of the spiritual power given to you by the Holy Spirit so that I may continue your ministry after you are gone." It was a godly request from a young man who loved his mentor.

To this request Elijah wisely replied that the power was not his to grant; the issue rested solely with God's sovereign will. No man can promise spiritual power to another. Only God can do that.

Yet the request was indeed granted. When Elisha picked up Elijah's cloak and struck the water of the Jordan River, he cried out, "Where now is the Lord, the God of Elijah?" (2 Kings 2:14) At those words, the waters parted, just as they had done earlier for Elijah. Seeing that, the prophets from Jericho correctly concluded that the spirit of Elijah had indeed been given to Elisha.

The secret of Elijah's ministry was the power of the Holy Spirit working in his life. When Elisha asked for the "double portion," he was asking that the same Holy Spirit work powerfully in his own life.

God granted Elisha's request because it came from a pure heart. If our motives are pure, we may freely ask God to do great things through us. God is honored when we seek the Holy Spirit's power in order to serve the Lord effectively.

Lord, as You poured out Your Spirit on the prophets of old, do it again in our day. Amen.

HAND OF GOD

Also in Judah the hand of God was on the people to give them unity of mind to carry out what the king and his officials had ordered, following the word of the Lord.
(2 Chronicles 30:12)

One of the greatest revivals of the Old Testament is recorded in 2 Chronicles 29–31. It happened when a godly king named Hezekiah repaired the temple doors and summoned the Levites to purify the house of God. He then reinstituted the yearly Passover celebration, even sending a letter inviting the northern tribes to come to Jerusalem to join in the observance. He told them not to be stubborn, but to return to the Lord who is gracious and full of compassion. Many people from the north ridiculed his offer, but some men humbled themselves and went to Jerusalem. At the same time, the "hand of God" was on the people of Judah, giving them unity of spirit to welcome their separated brethren from the north.

When all the people came together from north and south, they removed the pagan altars from Jerusalem and threw them in the Kidron Valley. Then all the people ate the Passover together. For seven days there was great rejoicing, so much so that the celebration was extended for another seven days. In 2 Chronicles 30:26, we find that "There was great joy in Jerusalem," for this was the first unified Passover since the days of King Solomon, some two hundred years earlier.

How did such a great reconciling event come about? Only because the "hand of God" stirred the people to come together in unity. It would never have happened otherwise. Ancient hostilities ran too deep; the memories of past separation kept the people of Israel and Judah from reaching out to each other. No edict of the king could have overcome the years of mistrust. Only the "hand of God" could bring the people together.

The Holy Spirit is the "hand of God" that changes hearts and minds from the inside out. Because He sees us as we are, because He knows us intimately, because He understands our fears, He can reach down within a closed heart and begin, little by little, to open it up. He is the only one who can overcome the fear built up through years of repeated injustice. His power can break down the walls that separate us from one another.

Spirit of God, You came to bring peace and unity in the body of Christ. May the hand of God bring us together and teach us to love one another. Amen.

YOUR GOOD SPIRIT

You gave your good Spirit to instruct them.
(Nehemiah 9:20)

The time: 445 B.C. The place: Jerusalem. The occasion: A day of repentance for the people of God. After Nehemiah led in rebuilding the wall around Jerusalem, Ezra led the nation in a time of spiritual renewal. Nehemiah 9 records a lengthy prayer by the Levites in which they recount the hand of God at work in the life of Israel across the generations. Despite the unbelief of the people, God had again and again shown Himself faithful.

Nehemiah 9:13–21 tells the story of God's faithfulness during the forty years in the wilderness. God gave the law and the sabbath (vv. 13–14) and sent manna from heaven and water from the rock (v. 15). He even forgave the people when they began to worship the golden calf (vv. 16–18). He led them with the cloud and pillar (v. 19), instructed them by His Spirit (v. 20), and sustained them for forty years in the desert so that they lacked for nothing (v. 21).

Verse 20 mentions "Your good Spirit" that instructed Israel in the wilderness. This may refer to those occasions in Exodus 28 and 31 where He gifted certain men who were helping to build the tabernacle and to design the priestly wardrobe. Or it may refer in a larger sense to all that God did during the wilderness experience to instruct Israel in the ways of holiness.

In any case we know that God's Spirit is a *good* Spirit. Because He is God, goodness is part of His character. All that He does is good and everything that He produces is good. Galatians 5:22 lists "goodness" as part of the fruit of the Spirit.

He is the same Spirit today because His nature is unchanged. He longs to produce in us the gracious generosity that the Bible calls goodness.

All He needs is a willing heart, and the Good Spirit of God will begin His gracious work in us.

Lord, how quickly I doubt Your goodness while traveling through the wilderness. Thank You for never leaving me even when I feel alone and overwhelmed. Amen.

YOUR SPIRIT

By your Spirit you admonished them through your prophets. (Nehemiah 9:30)

This verse refers to all the prophets of Israel who faithfully warned the nation of coming judgment. It includes Elijah, Elisha, Isaiah, Jeremiah, Hosea, Amos, and a host of other godly men who courageously spoke God's Word to an uncaring nation.

How did these men find the strength to carry on in a society that had chosen to reject God? They knew ahead of time that their words would be largely disregarded and they themselves would be rejected, hated, persecuted, and sometimes put to death. Being a prophet was not a good career choice in ancient Israel. It was much easier to be a baker or a farmer or a shepherd.

No one likes being rejected. Most people would rather be loved and appreciated. The only possible explanation for the prophets of Israel is that they had been called by God and empowered by God to deliver His Word.

Jeremiah spoke of the Word being like a fire in his bones that he could not hold in any longer (Jeremiah 20:9). The prophets often mentioned a "burden" from the Lord. When God calls us, He also puts a passion in our hearts for the thing He has called us to do.

This is the work of the Holy Spirit. He gives us the supernatural strength to do God's will in the face of unrelenting opposition. Are we in a similar situation today? Fear not. The Holy Spirit will provide us with strength when we really need it.

Spirit of God, give holy zeal to Your servants today. May Your people speak Your truth without fear of the consequences. Set me afire with holy desire to do Your will. Amen.

THE BREATH OF THE ALMIGHTY

But it is the spirit in a man, the breath of the Almighty, that gives him understanding. (Job 32:8)

The Spirit of God has made me; the breath of the Almighty gives me life. (Job 33:4)

If it were his intention and he withdrew his Spirit and breath, all mankind would perish. (Job 34:14–15)

These verses clearly teach the deity of the Holy Spirit. He is the very breath of the Almighty. In contrast with certain doctrines that downplay the Holy Spirit or relegate Him to a role less than equal with God, Elihu (the speaker in all three passages) asserts the role of the Holy Spirit in creation, giving and sustaining life, and giving understanding. Without the Holy Spirit, all mankind would promptly perish. This high view of the Holy Spirit is only possible if He is indeed the third member of the Holy Trinity, equal in position and power to the Father and the Son.

These verses also stress the sovereign power of the Spirit. We owe our very lives to Him. Even unbelievers owe their existence to the Spirit of God. He demonstrates His grace to us by granting us life and breath this very moment.

The "understanding" that the Holy Spirit gives goes beyond the wisdom that comes with age and experience. Through the Holy Spirit, even young men and women may possess insight into life that those much older will never attain.

Breath of God, I bow before Your awesome power. Sweep through me, renew me, give me wisdom beyond my years. Amen.

Do not cast me from your presence or take your Holy Spirit from me. (Psalm 51:11)

King David penned these famous words in the aftermath of his disastrous affair with Bathsheba. Adultery led to a cover-up which eventually led to murder and the death of a newborn baby. In fact, that one sin led to the eventual crumbling of his empire and the slow disintegration of his family.

When he finally reached the bottom, David cried out to God from the depths of humiliation and utter despair. Psalm 51 is perhaps the clearest picture in all the Bible of what true repentance looks like. There are no excuses, there is no passing the buck, no pleading of extenuating circumstances. "For I know my transgressions, and my sin is always before me" (v. 3). When he finally came to his senses David saw clearly that his basic sin was treason against God. Adultery was simply the outward expression of inward mutiny against the Lord. In the end David agreed with God's judgment on his sin and confessed how deeply sin had stained his life (vv. 4–6). He begged to be forgiven and cleansed from the inside out (v. 7–9). Then he asked for a miracle: "Create in me a pure heart, O God, and renew a steadfast spirit within me" (v. 10). It was a prayer that only God could answer.

That brings us to verse 11 where he prayed not to be cast out from God's presence and asked that the Holy Spirit not be taken from him. Did David fear losing his salvation? No, probably not in the sense we use the term today. The kings of ancient Israel all knew that God had placed them on the throne and anointed them with the presence and power of the Holy Spirit. Perhaps David recalled Saul's experience. When Saul was anointed by Samuel, the Holy Spirit came upon him and Saul was changed into a "different person" (1 Samuel 10:6–7). This experience evidently gave Saul an unusual measure of spiritual power that enabled him to rule Israel successfully. Later on, because of his disobedience, the Lord rejected him as king and the Holy Spirit departed from Saul, to be replaced by "an evil spirit from the Lord." All this happened at the time when Samuel anointed David and the Holy Spirit came upon him (1 Samuel 16:13–14).

Did David remember what happened to Saul? How could he forget the sudden, violent changes in personality, the mood swings, the friendship that turned to murderous hatred? David understood that once the Holy Spirit left Saul, he was never the same again.

In Psalm 51:11, David prayed that what happened to Saul might not happen to him. It is a prayer related to the empowerment of the Spirit for continued service as the king of Israel. Having seen what happened to Saul, David knew that if the Holy Spirit left him, he too would be effectively finished as the ruler of Israel.

A similar New Testament passage might be 1 Corinthians 9:24–27, where Paul says that he disciplined his body lest after preaching to others he would become "disqualified"—useless to God and man, put on the shelf and disqualified from further service.

It is sometimes said that a New Testament believer could never pray this prayer today. But I'm not sure that is correct. Could the blessing of God be removed from a sinning believer? Yes. Could the Holy Spirit's empowerment be taken away? Yes. Could a born-again Christian sin so grievously that he or she is "disqualified" from further effective service? If the answer is yes, then David's prayer would indeed be appropriate.

In any case, let us all be warned from David's example. If such a man as he could sin so terribly and hurt so many people, if he could legitimately fear that the Holy Spirit's empowerment might be removed from his life, then the same thing might happen to us as well.

Let us heed the solemn words of 1 Corinthians 10:12, "If you think you are standing firm, be careful that you don't fall!"

Lord Jesus, may I never take Your blessings for granted or feel that I have advanced so far that sin cannot touch me, lest what happened to others should also happen to me. Amen.

YOUR SPIRIT OF
CREATION AND RENEWAL

When you send your Spirit, they are created, and you renew the face of the earth. (Psalm 104:30)

Psalm 104 is a magnificent hymn in praise of God's creation. Verses 1–23 praise the Creator who brought all things into being. Verses 24–32 praise the Lord for His sovereignty over the earth. He made the earth and its creatures in all their various forms, including the land animals and the creatures of the sea (vv. 24–26). All these living things look to God for their food (vv. 27–28). They owe their very existence to God's Spirit (vv. 29–30). The Psalmist prays that the glory of the Lord might endure since He controls every part of creation (vv. 31–32).

Verse 30 tells us two things about the work of the Holy Spirit: (1) all creatures are created by the Spirit; (2) the earth itself is renewed by the Spirit. Thus we learn that even the animals owe their continued existence to the work of the Holy Spirit.

The original creation was completed in the first six days of the world but in another sense, creation continues every day through the ongoing work of the Holy Spirit in the world. As the seasons change, God through His Spirit renews the world, sending forth the rain and sun to renew the face of the earth.

Psalm 104:30 brings before us an expansive, exalted view of the Holy Spirit. We make a vast mistake if we think that the Holy Spirit's work is limited only to salvation. True, that is where His work is most clearly seen, but the Old Testament teaches us that the Spirit has been at work in the world from the very beginning.

All praise and glory to You, Sovereign Lord, for sending Your Spirit into the world. How vast are Your works, how magnificent Your plans, how gracious is Your care for the world You made. Amen.

YOUR PRESENCE

*Where can I go from your Spirit? Where can I
flee from your presence?* (Psalm 139:7)

Theologians speak of the "omnipresence" of God.
That means He is everywhere-present at all times
and in all situations. Perhaps no other passage so
clearly illustrates this truth as does Psalm 139:7–12.
David began to imagine places where he might go
to be totally separated from God's Spirit. Perhaps
he could go to the highest point or the lowest
depths (v. 8); or perhaps he could go east or west
to the far side of the most distant ocean (vv. 9–10);
or perhaps he could find some hiding place in the
darkness where God could not find him (vv. 11–12).

The answer in every case is negative—or perhaps we should actually say it is positive. Since
God is present everywhere, there is nowhere we
can go to be hidden from Him. He is there at the
highest point and the lowest depth (v. 8). His hand
holds us fast on the other side of the earth (v. 10).
No one can hide from God in the darkness because "darkness is as light" to Him (v. 12).

This thought is both comforting and frightening
—comforting because no matter how desperate
our circumstances, God's Spirit will never leave
us; frightening because no matter how much we
try to free ourselves from God's oversight, His Spirit
is with us wherever we go.

Is this good news or bad news? Ultimately, it's
good news because a world without God's Spirit

would be a world where no one could survive for even one day. It's also good news because it means that no matter where we are geographically or spiritually, God's Spirit is not far away. He's right there with us. Even as we read these words, God's Spirit is by our side.

Think of it. God knows us through and through. He formed us in the womb before we were born. And His Spirit is with us wherever we go.

Spirit of God, since there is nowhere I can go to flee from You, teach me to live each moment in the awareness that You are always with me. Amen.

THE LAMP OF THE LORD

*The lamp of the Lord searches the spirit of a
man; it searches out his inmost being.*
(Proverbs 20:27)

What is meant by "the lamp of the Lord?" Some
commentators believe it refers to the human conscience, which "searches out" a man's motive,
helping discern between good and evil. However,
it is more likely a reference to the Holy Spirit, who
like a bright lamp goes from one "room" of the
heart to another, searching out those things that
even conscience cannot discover. After all, a man
may have a "seared conscience" and be a moral
sociopath, totally unable to know right from wrong.
Conscience is a good guide, but it is not infallible.
But the Holy Spirit sees and knows every thought
and intent of the heart. Nothing is hidden from
Him. Like a blazing light, the Spirit of God exposes everything, sees everything, drags the deepest secrets out of the closet and exposes them to
the light of God. Proverbs 5:21 speaks of the same
truth, "For a man's ways are in full view of the
Lord, and He examines all his paths." To that we
might add Proverbs 15:3, "The eyes of the Lord are
everywhere, keeping watch on the wicked and the
good."

Once again, we find a truth about the Holy Spirit
that is both comforting and terrifying. To those
who have nothing to hide, the lamp of the Lord
holds no fear; but to those who have many "hid-

den things," the lamp of the Lord brings them all to the light sooner or later.

How should we then live? Since the lamp of Lord constantly searches our inmost being, let us live openly, honestly, hiding nothing. Then we will have nothing to fear as the Holy Spirit searches us out.

Lamp of the Lord, search me, cleanse me, move within me until nothing is hidden and all things are laid bare before You. Amen.

SPIRIT OF JUDGMENT AND FIRE

He will cleanse the bloodstains from Jerusalem
by a spirit of judgment and a spirit of fire.
(Isaiah 4:4)

The prophet Isaiah, though speaking 2,700 years ago, prophesies concerning events yet future to us. In Isaiah 4, we find a description of the terrible events that will engulf Israel during the tribulation period prior to the return of Christ to the earth. Those seven awful years will climax with the battle of Armageddon and the return of Christ to the earth (Revelation 19). So great will be the human slaughter that most men will be killed. But those who survive will see the Lord as He returns to set up His kingdom. His reign will bring great bounty to the Holy Land and great blessing to Jerusalem (Isaiah 4:2–3).

But the people of Israel still must be cleansed from their sin of unbelief and rebellion against God. And the land itself must be consecrated again because it will be polluted from the final battle. Verse 4 speaks of the fire of coming judgment that will cleanse the bloodstains from Jerusalem and purify it in preparation for the coming kingdom of Christ. That "spirit of fire" will be the Holy Spirit cleansing the land from its sin. Once that purification is complete, the glory of the Lord will once again dwell in the land (vv. 5–6).

The same "spirit of fire" works to purify the people of God today. Before revival must come repentance. Before repentance must come confession. Before confession must come conviction. But conviction of sin is the unique ministry of the Holy Spirit.

He must "burn" within us until we are willing to face up to our sin. No one likes to do that. Hiding and denying seem much more comfortable. But a red face and a few hot tears will go a long way to bring us back to God.

How long has it been since you felt the "burning" of the Spirit in your heart? If you can't remember, perhaps it's time for you to get alone with God and let the "spirit of fire" do His work in your life.

O Holy Spirit, burn within me until I come clean with You. Amen.

SPIRIT OF WISDOM
AND UNDERSTANDING

The Spirit of the Lord will rest on him—the
Spirit of wisdom and of understanding.
(Isaiah 11:2)

Isaiah referred more to the Holy Spirit than any
other Old Testament prophet. In this passage, he
predicts that the fullness of the Holy Spirit will rest
on the Messiah, Jesus Christ, the "shoot" that will
come up from the "stump of Jesse." In those days,
Assyria had nearly destroyed Judah, cutting it down
to the size of a stump. Though Assyria and her al-
lies seemed like a mighty forest, the Lord promised that He would one day cut them all down
(Isaiah 10:33–34). The Assyrian empire would fall,
to be replaced by another one much greater—the
worldwide empire of the Messiah.

But where will the Messiah come from? He will
be a tiny shoot from the forgotten stump of Jesse
(father of David). Just as God had promised in
2 Samuel 7, a descendant of David would rule
over the house of Israel forever. Though it seemed
unlikely at the time, God's ultimate ruler would indeed come from Judah, from the very line of David.
Isaiah predicted that Christ would be a "Branch"
bearing fruit, that is, a ruler who would prosper
and benefit many people. A few verses later (11:10),
Isaiah called Him the "Root of Jesse." Christ is
therefore the tender shoot who is also the Root
who is also the Branch.

Isaiah 11:2–3 predicts that the Spirit of the Lord will rest on Christ. Three couplets are used to describe the Holy Spirit: He is the "Spirit of wisdom and of understanding, the Spirit of counsel and of power, the Spirit of knowledge and of the fear of the Lord."

The first couplet speaks of the Holy Spirit's gift of wisdom and understanding. "Wisdom" refers to practical insight for living while "understanding" has the idea of keen judgment. To have both wisdom and understanding means not only that we have insight into the problems of life; it also implies the ability to make good decisions in response to those problems. Both of these characteristics may be seen in the life of Christ. When He met the woman at the well (John 4), He understood her true need ("living water") and the sordid past that held her back ("You have had five husbands, and the man you now have is not your husband"). He also understood the deeper issue that separated the Samaritans and the Jews. (The proper place for worship was a long-term source of debate between the two peoples.) Finally, Jesus pointed her to the truth that since God is spirit, the place of worship is irrelevant ("His worshipers must worship in spirit and in truth"). Only when those issues were laid to rest did He reveal Himself as the Messiah ("I who speak to you am He.") Thus He led the woman step by step away from her ignorance and to true faith in Himself.

We will experience growth in wisdom and understanding as we rely on the Holy Spirit. He will give us practical insight into the problems of life. He will also give us the ability to make wise decisions.

We can count on it because He is "the Spirit of wisdom and of understanding."

Lord, without You I am like a lost child wandering through the streets. Send Your Spirit to show me the way I should go. Amen.

SPIRIT OF COUNSEL AND POWER

The Spirit of the Lord will rest on him ... the Spirit of counsel and of power. (Isaiah 11:2)

The second couplet speaks of moral insight and heroic purpose. Note the relation to Christ's title in Isaiah 9:6, "He will be called Wonderful Counselor"—when He speaks, people will gladly listen. Matthew 7:28–29 tells us that when Jesus spoke, the crowds were amazed "because He taught as one who had authority, and not as their teachers of the law" who continually quoted other rabbis.

We often think of Christ's power solely in terms of miracles such as healing the sick, casting out demons, making the lame walk, and raising the dead. These things do indeed demonstrate the "Spirit of power" that was upon Him. However, there are other kinds of power besides working spectacular miracles. For instance, power enabled Jesus to walk through a hostile crowd (Luke 4:14–30), to cleanse the temple at Jerusalem (Matthew 21:12–13), to condemn the Pharisees publicly (Matthew 23), to calmly face His accusers without uttering an angry word (Matthew 26:62–63), and to forgive those who crucified Him even as He hung on the cross (Luke 23:34).

The same Holy Spirit who gave Christ such awesome courage now dwells in us!

Spirit of God, fill me with Your power so that I may speak when I need to speak and be silent when nothing more needs to be said. Amen.

SPIRIT OF KNOWLEDGE
AND OF THE FEAR OF THE LORD

*The Spirit of the Lord will rest on him ... the
Spirit of knowledge and of the fear of the Lord.*
(Isaiah 11:2)

The third couplet relates to knowing God and doing
His will. "Knowledge" is more than the accumula-
tion of facts. It refers to the intimate understanding of God and His eternal purposes in the world.
To "know" God is to enter into a deep, intimate,
personal relationship with Him. Speaking of Christ,
Psalm 40:8 says, "I desire to do Your will, O my
God; Your law is within my heart." Jesus didn't
come to earth with His own personal agenda; He
came to fulfill God's will. When Jesus prayed with
His disciples just hours before He was arrested,
He said to the Father, "I have brought You glory
on earth by completing the work You gave me to
do" (John 17:4).

Knowing God's will is one thing; doing it is
something else. More than anyone who ever lived,
Jesus could say, "I have completely done God's
will." That's the implication of the second phrase
—"The Spirit ... of the fear of the Lord." Jesus
could truthfully say, "I always do what pleases
Him." To fear the Lord is to respect Him so much
that we adjust all our words, thoughts, and deeds
so that they truly please God.

If we take these six descriptions together, we
have a picture of the perfect ruler:

He has the ability to understand the problems of life.

He knows how to make wise decisions that help people.

He speaks in such a way that others want to listen.

He shows heroic grace under pressure.

He knows God deeply and intimately.

He truly pleases God in all that He does.

That is what Isaiah means when he says, "The Spirit of the Lord will rest on Him" (Isaiah 11:2). In contrast to the long line of failed kings of Israel and Judah, God promised to send a man who would be perfectly controlled by the Spirit of God.

Seven hundred years later He did. The promise was fulfilled in the Babe born in Bethlehem—unseen and unnoticed by the world—was the "shoot" from the stump of Jesse. He was the Branch who would bear fruit for the entire world.

They called Him Jesus—"Savior"—but He was also the Root and Branch promised long before by Isaiah.

He came in the power of the Holy Spirit. He lived in the power of the Spirit. He died and rose again in the power of the Spirit.

He not only showed us what God is like. He also showed us what it means to be fully dependent on the power of the Spirit.

If we want to see a truly Spirit-filled man, we will look at Jesus.

Father, thank You for giving me such a clear example of the Spirit-filled life. Help me today to follow in Jesus' steps. Amen.

SPIRIT OF JUSTICE

He will be a spirit of justice to him who sits in judgment, a source of strength to those who turn back the battle at the gate. (Isaiah 28:6)

Isaiah 28 prophesies the fall of Samaria, the proud and intoxicated capital of the northern kingdom of Israel. The Lord will come with the force of a driving hailstorm and throw the city to the ground (v. 2). He will use the Assyrians to attack Samaria. They will gobble up the city as a man eagerly eats a ripe fig (v. 4). That awful judgment will lead many people to return to the Lord, who "will be a glorious crown, a beautiful wreath for the remnant of His people" (v. 5). Those who are brought to their senses by God's judgment will discover that the Lord is a "spirit of justice." The judges who up till this time had been corrupt and greedy will find that when the Lord takes over, He sends a spirit of justice to correct wrongdoing.

No more trampling on the rights of the poor!
No more robbing widow's houses!
No more taking bribes!
No more mistreating the aliens!
No more charging exorbitant interest!
No more shedding innocent blood!

The Old Testament is filled with warnings about injustice. The message comes through loud and clear: Our God is a God of justice! He will not stand idly by while His people act unjustly.

As we think about it, let's remember that justice is the reason God sent His Son into the world. Sin offends God's justice, and He could not forgive sin without satisfying His own justice. Therefore, He sent His own Son to die for our sins—the just for the unjust—that He might bring us to God.

Justice matters to God! When we work for justice, in a very real sense we are working for God. When we roll up our sleeves and get involved in the hurts of this ugly world, we may know with certainty that the "spirit of justice" will be with us.

Father, may I not be blind to the injustice all around me. Rouse me by Your Spirit to do something about it. Amen.

THE SPIRIT FROM ON HIGH

Till the Spirit is poured upon us from on high.
(Isaiah 32:15)

Suddenly Isaiah pressed the "fast-forward" button. The scene is the end of time when Christ returns to set up His kingdom on the earth (Isaiah 32:1). Egypt and Assyria have been left far behind. A new world comes into focus. In that day, justice will fill the earth (vv. 1–2), spiritual disabilities will be removed (vv. 3–5), both sinners and the righteous will be seen for what they really are (vv. 6–8), and the time of blessing will be preceded by painful judgment (vv. 9–14).

Then the Spirit will be poured out on the earth. Like rain falling from the skies, the Holy Spirit will fill the earth during the millennial reign of Christ. The result will be fertile fields (v. 15), widespread righteousness (v. 16), and peace on earth (vv. 17–19).

It is obvious that these things have not yet happened. There is too much hunger, too much poverty, too much injustice, and too little peace. Indeed, these things *cannot* happen without the personal presence of the King who reigns in righteousness—Jesus Christ.

In that day, the Spirit will be poured out as never before. Though the present age is sometimes called "the Age of the Spirit," the coming kingdom of Christ will be far more marvelous. Whereas there is currently much opposition to the work of the

Spirit (because of sin in the world), in that day the Holy Spirit will be "unleashed" to bless the earth with His gracious presence.

Jesus will be the King. But the Holy Spirit will be there too. The Son will reign from His throne in Jerusalem, and the Spirit will work His wonders across the whole earth.

Be encouraged, child of God. Better days are coming.

Father, thank You for the "blessed hope" of Christ's return. I say with the people of God across the centuries, "Even so, come Lord Jesus." Amen.

The grass withers and the flowers fall, because the breath of the Lord blows on them. Surely the people are grass. (Isaiah 40:7)

In the King James Version, the last phrase of verse 7 is translated as "because the Spirit of the Lord blows on them." It's the Hebrew word *ruah*, which may be translated as "breath" or "spirit." I am inclined to translate this verse using the word "Spirit" because as many other passages make clear, the Holy Spirit *is* the Breath of the Lord.

The emphasis on this passage is the frailty of man versus the enduring character of God's Word. People come and go. They are born, live, die, and slowly fade from memory. If you doubt that, visit any cemetery. The frozen headstones tell the story of men and women who lived and died and now are mostly forgotten. If they died more than a few years ago, there is probably no one around who knew them or even knew they existed.

Such is the nature of life . . . and death. No one lives forever. We are like the grass of the field. Or a beautiful cut flower. Today, the grass seems lush and green. The flower blazes in full bloom. But tomorrow morning, the grass has started to wither and the flower has lost its sheen. By the day after tomorrow, the grass has withered away and the flower has faded into shriveled petals.

Such is all life on earth—including your life and mine. We grow old, we wither, we fade, and sooner or later, we pass off the scene. It happens because the "breath of God" blows upon us. It is the "breath of God" that gives life; it is the "breath of God" that takes life away. So it is that we owe our very existence to God the Holy Spirit. He breathes, and life comes into us. He breathes again, and life is taken away.

Against the frailty of man stands the unchanging Word of God. We come and go; the Word of God stands forever. The generations roll on, the cemeteries take in new tenants, but God's Word endures forever.

In what shall we trust? In the feeble works of man? In the perishing products of perishing people? No, because this world and all that is in it is passing. If we are wise, we will build our lives on the Word of God, the only thing that will outlast this fading world.

Thank You for reminding me again how frail I really am. Help me to build my life on those things that will last forever. Amen.

THE MIND OF THE LORD

Who has understood the mind of the Lord, or instructed him as his counselor? (Isaiah 40:13)

The New International Version translates *ruah* as "the mind" of the Lord, perhaps in consideration of Paul's use of this verse in Romans 11:34. In any case, the meaning is quite clear. Isaiah is speaking of the greatness of God. Isaiah 40:1–11 speaks of God's power to deliver His people from captivity. This great deliverance will happen because "the Sovereign Lord comes with power" (v. 10). Verses 12–31 shift the focus to the greatness of God in creation. These verses stress how majestic and exalted is the Lord. Verses 12–14 ask five rhetorical questions, all of which expect the answer, "no one."

Who has marked off the universe with His fingers? "No one."

Who has held the earth in His hands? "No one."

Who fully understands what God intends to do? "No one."

Whom did the Lord ask for advice? "No one."

Who taught God things He never knew? "No one."

The third question could be translated this way: "Who can give advice to the Spirit of the Lord?" The answer is, "No one can." No mortal man regulates the Holy Spirit for He is truly the "mind of the Lord."

Behind this verse stands the doctrine of the omniscience of God. Because He truly knows all that was, is, will be, and even all things that could be, He needs no instruction from anyone else. Since there is no lack in His knowledge, no one needs to tell the Lord what He needs to do.

Who has ever told God's Spirit what He should do? No one, and it is folly to try. We may bow before the Spirit of God or we may fight against Him. But let no one make the mistake of instructing the Holy Spirit. We can't do it, so we shouldn't waste our time.

When the Holy Spirit speaks, God speaks, for the Spirit of God is truly the mind of the Lord.

God our Father, You spoke and the universe came into being. You did not need my help nor could I have improved on Your work. I bow before Your greatness. Amen.

For I will pour water on the thirsty land, and streams on the dry ground. I will pour out my Spirit on your offspring, and my blessing on your descendants. (Isaiah 44:3)

In Isaiah 44, the prophet reached far into the future to describe a day of great blessing for Israel. After judgment would come a regathering to the land. With the regathering would come an outpouring of the Holy Spirit. Although in Isaiah's day, Israel seemed like a parched desert, when Christ returns, the Spirit will flow so freely that the nation will seem like cold mountain streams covering the hot sand. Where once there was no water —only dry, dusty, mud-baked hardness—the Holy Spirit will come with such power that the land will break out in lush vegetation.

In this case, the "land" stands for the people of God. *They* are the parched ground; *they* are the dry desert; *they* have been thirsty so long that they have forgotten what it feels like to take a drink of cool water.

God said to His thirsty people, "I will pour out My Spirit and give you rivers of cool water to drink."

The literal fulfillment of Isaiah 44 awaits the second coming of Jesus Christ when He will restore the fortunes of Israel and establish His throne in Jerusalem. Then the nation will enjoy the Holy Spirit in a way it never has before.

But there is a present fulfillment of these verses for everyone who seeks the Holy Spirit. Jesus spoke in John 7:37–39 about the "streams of living water" that would flow forth from those who believe in Him. Without in the slightest way canceling the promises made to Israel, Jesus extended the blessing of the Spirit to all His followers, Jews and Gentiles alike.

Have you ever felt like spiritually "dry ground"? Have you ever felt "thirsty" for more of the Lord? Have you ever felt empty and needing to be filled?

The Holy Spirit is God's answer for our deep inner thirst. When He comes into our lives, He comes like a river rushing over dry ground. He pours out His blessings and our lives begin to blossom again.

No one need stay "dry" or "empty" or "thirsty" forever. We weren't made to live in a desert. God's river called the Holy Spirit can flow through our lives, slaking our thirst, filling our emptiness, covering the arid ground with the water of life.

Spirit of God, I am thirsty until You flow through me. I am empty until You fill me. I am dry until You cause life to spring up once again. Do it, now! Amen.

HIS SPIRIT

And now the Sovereign Lord has sent me, with his Spirit. (Isaiah 48:16)

Here is one of the unique verses of the Old Testament. It is one of the few verses that mentions all three members of the Trinity—Father, Son, and Holy Spirit:

The Sovereign Lord—The Father
Has sent me—The Son
With His Spirit—The Holy Spirit

Dr. Charles Ryrie calls this "an Old Testament glimpse of the Trinity." As such, it answers those who say that the Trinity is strictly a New Testament doctrine.

In the larger context, this verse contrasts Cyrus (conqueror of Babylon) with the Servant of the Lord, the Messiah, who will also accomplish His mission. When He comes to redeem the nations, He will offer Himself as the perfect sacrifice, taking upon Himself "the iniquity of us all" (Isaiah 53:6). Sent by the Father and aided by the Spirit, the Son will not fail as the "Redeemer, the Holy One of Israel" (Isaiah 48:17).

What does this tell us about the Holy Spirit? He is truly God just as much as the Father and the Son. He is not less than God or some kind of "impersonal influence." He who is the Spirit of God is truly God the Holy Spirit, possessing all the attributes of deity, worthy of worship, praise, and prayer, and demanding from us complete submission and obedience.

Never make the mistake of taking the Holy Spirit lightly. When He speaks, God speaks. When He calls, God calls. When we resist Him, we are actually resisting God.

As Christians throughout the ages have declared, our God eternally exists in three persons—Father, Son, and Holy Spirit.

Spirit of God, I worship You not as some angelic being or mystical influence, but as You are—very God of very God. Amen.

SPIRIT OF THE SOVEREIGN LORD

*The Spirit of the Sovereign Lord is on me,
because the Lord anointed me to preach good
news to the poor.* (Isaiah 61:1)

This extremely important passage was quoted by
Jesus in Luke 4:18, on the occasion of His sermon
in the synagogue at Nazareth. He also alluded to it
in His reply to the disciples of John the Baptist in
Matthew 11:4–6. In both cases, Jesus was claim-
ing that Isaiah 61:1–2 was fulfilled in Him.

Once again we should note that the Trinity is
clearly implied in verse 1:

The Spirit—Holy Spirit
Of the Sovereign Lord—the Father
Is on me—The Son

This passage tells us what things will character-
ize Messiah's ministry: (1) preaching the Gospel
to the poor; (2) binding up the brokenhearted;
(3) freedom for the captives; (4) release from the
darkness. In verse 2, Isaiah tells us that he will
proclaim the grace of God ("the year of the Lord's
favor") and will warn of coming judgment ("the
day of vengeance of our God"). All these things
were fulfilled in the ministry of Jesus Christ.

For our purposes, we should note that Jesus ful-
filled His ministry in the power of the Holy Spirit.
He did not act of His own accord (though He
Himself was God), but fully depended on the Holy
Spirit because He was the perfect pattern of what
humanity could be. Although He was the Son of

61

God and possessed the full attributes of deity, He was "anointed" with the Spirit in order to do His ministry. In the power of the Spirit, He proclaimed freedom from the captivity of sin .

Such is the power of the Holy Spirit that even the Son of God relied on Him to do His work. Not because Jesus could not do it Himself, but because He meant to leave us a pattern for our own lives. If Christ depended upon the Holy Spirit, how much more should we?

It is said that the great evangelist Billy Sunday began every sermon by opening his Bible to Isaiah 61 and placing his notes on this text. Thus did He remind himself that the power for life-changing ministry comes only from the Holy Spirit.

Spirit of God, anoint me today for the preaching of Gospel. Empower me to proclaim liberty to those trapped in the jailhouse of sin. As I share the Good News, may Your Spirit give life to my words. Amen.

*Yet they rebelled and grieved his Holy Spirit. So
he turned and became their enemy. Where is he
who set his Holy Spirit among them?*
(Isaiah 63:10–11)

In this section of Isaiah, the prophet prayed that
God might speedily bring about the redemption of
Israel. As he prayed, Isaiah recalled God's great
mercy to the Israelites in past generations, focus-
ing on the deliverance from Egypt and the wandering in the wilderness.

But all was not well with God's people. After
they left Egypt, they rebelled against God, complaining about their living conditions and how
much they had left behind on the other side of the
Red Sea. It is possible that Isaiah has Numbers 20
in mind, where the people complained bitterly
about their lack of water at Kadesh in the Desert of
Zin. They even said to Moses that it would have
been better to have died in the desert or remained
in Egypt than to have come to "this terrible place."

In response, God told Moses to speak to the
rock and it would pour forth water. Moses, en-
raged by the rebellious, ungrateful attitude of the
people, instead struck the rock twice, in disobedience to the Lord's command, for which sin he was
barred from entering the Holy Land.

The whole scene is a sad commentary on the
spiritual state of Israel and also upon Moses' lack
of self-control. But it wasn't the first time Israel

had complained. Almost from the very beginning of the wilderness journey, the people had grumbled against the Lord.

This ungrateful attitude "grieved" the Holy Spirit (the only time this phrase is used in the Old Testament). Here we learn that the Holy Spirit is a Person with the capacity for grief, not simply an influence or power. We learn also that an ungrateful heart grieves the Holy Spirit of God. Stubborn rebellion leads to the uncomfortable place where God becomes the enemy of His own people.

Could such a thing happen today? One need only think of Ananias and Sapphira (Acts 5:1–11) and the case of the Corinthian believers who defiled the Lord's Supper in 1 Corinthians 11:25–32.

The Holy Spirit is indeed our Comforter and the Christian's best friend, but we must never forget that He is truly the *Holy* Spirit, who will not wink at sin or overlook a rebellious attitude.

He didn't do it back then. He won't do it now.

The best solution is to live in such a way that we never grieve the Holy Spirit in the first place.

Spirit of God, search my heart and bring to light the tiniest seeds of an ungrateful spirit. Then grant me grace to remove those seeds before they bear bitter fruit in my life. Amen.

THE SPIRIT WHO GIVES REST

Like cattle that go down to the plain, they were given rest by the Spirit of the Lord.
(Isaiah 63:14)

Here is the other side of the truth just mentioned. We may indeed grieve the Holy Spirit, but that does not mean that God gives up on us. Israel's history shows again and again how the people failed the Lord, were punished for their sin, and then returned to the Lord who restored their fortunes.

Isaiah recalls the fact that God's grace extended to Israel even after their repeated rebellion. Though the people sinned repeatedly, God never gave up on them, but in His judgment, He remembered mercy.

Eventually Israel did indeed enter the Promised Land, a land flowing with milk and honey, a land so wonderful that it seemed as if there were horses running free in the countryside or cattle who had found a level plain for grazing. Many battles still lay ahead of them, years of conquest and settlement. But as Joshua 21:44 notes, "The Lord gave them rest on every side, just as he had sworn to their forefathers." All their enemies were defeated by the good hand of God. God had not failed on a single promise.

Thus, the Holy Spirit of God led His people from Egypt, through the desert, and into the Promised Land. It wasn't easy or quick. In fact, it took about forty years longer than Moses had planned. But in the end, despite many false starts, mistakes, setbacks, and disappointments, and despite unending complaints, doubts, and outright rebellion against God, the Lord led His people into "rest."

John Newton's famous hymn "Amazing Grace" contains a verse that seems to apply at this point:

Through many dangers, toils and snares,
I have already come.
'Tis grace hath brought me safe thus far,
And grace will lead me home.

Cheer up, Christian. It is God's intention to give you "rest." You may not see it or sense it or feel it, but even now, God's Spirit is at work leading you from a place of strife to a place of calm and peaceful rest.

We'll never "rest" fully until we get to heaven, but even in the midst of our current struggles, God wants to give us rest.

When we stay close to the Lord and rely on His Spirit, step by step, slowly but surely, He will give us rest.

Spirit of God, I am weary and need the rest You have promised. As You gave rest to Your people in days past, so lead me now to the "level plain" where I can find rest for my soul. Amen.

A NEW SPIRIT

I will give them an undivided heart and put a new spirit in them. (Ezekiel 11:19)

Many of the Old Testament prophets looked forward to a day when God would transform His people from the inside out. Jeremiah spoke of the "new covenant" that God would someday establish with Israel. Isaiah looked forward to a day when the Spirit would never depart from the people of God. Hosea and Micah looked for a day when God's forgiveness would be complete. Amos connected that day with the regathering of Israel. Zechariah saw that these things could not ultimately be fulfilled without the coming of the Lord.

Ezekiel 11:19–20 describes the work of the Holy Spirit in transforming the human heart. The new covenant provides a new allegiance to God and the indwelling of the Holy Spirit. By a work of God's grace, Israel would receive a "heart of flesh" (meaning a heart responsive to God) in place of a "heart of stone" (meaning a hard heart that is spiritually dead). Two results flow from this "divine heart transplant": a new obedience to God and a new relationship with God (v. 20).

Though this new covenant was made with Israel, Hebrews 8–10 tells us that those same blessings are now extended to everyone who believes in Jesus Christ. The land-related promises made to Israel will yet be fulfilled when Christ returns to set up His kingdom. In the meantime, the spiritual blessings of the new covenant are freely given to all believers—Jew and Gentile alike.

What an enormous miracle this is. What we could not do for ourselves (truly change our basic nature), God has done through the work of the Holy Spirit. Where once we struggled and failed because we had "hearts of stone," now God has given us a "new heart" and a "new spirit."

Alexander Pope is said to have muttered to himself one day, "Lord, make me a better man." His servant replied, "It would be easier to make you a new man."

But only God can do that. He sends the Holy Spirit who changes us from the inside out. He makes "new men" and "new women" by performing spiritual heart transplants.

God does this every time a person trusts Christ. The moment we are born again, the Holy Spirit gives us a brand-new heart, one that loves God and truly desires to keep His commandments.

What we couldn't do in a million years, God does for us instantly through the power of the Spirit.

Father, thank You for doing the impossible. You change me when I think I could never be changed. Thank You for going far beyond my small expectations. Amen.

DEW

I will be like the dew to Israel. (Hosea 14:5)

Dew in the Bible often symbolizes God's blessings. When Isaac blessed Jacob in Genesis 27:28, he prayed, "May God give you of heaven's dew." Moses pronounced the same blessing upon Joseph in Deuteronomy 33:13 and used the same imagery in 33:28 to describe the blessedness of the Promised Land ("a land of grain and new wine, where the heavens drop dew"). Psalm 133:3 uses dew as a sign of rich bounty and fruitfulness. Isaiah 26:19 uses the phrase "dew of the morning" to describe the resurrection from the dead.

All these verses use dew to represent fruitfulness, freshness, and unlimited bounty. When the Lord says in Hosea 14:5, "I will be like the dew to Israel," He means that when the nation repents and returns to the Lord, it will experience an untold outpouring of blessing from heaven. It will be like the blossoming of the lily (14:5).

The Holy Spirit is God's "dew from heaven." Through the Spirit, God pours out His blessings on the earth. It is the Holy Spirit who brings us all the blessings of God day by day. As the dew comes fresh every morning, even so we daily experience the riches of heaven. "They are new every morning" (Lamentations 3:23).

Dew also reminds us how the Holy Spirit works —quietly, softly, gently, without public announcement or great fanfare. He doesn't call attention to

Himself. He silently refreshes the earth with His ministry.

Day by day, the Holy Spirit delights to bring the things of God to us. Tomorrow morning, why not start the day by thanking God for the faithfulness of His Spirit?

Lord God, in my busyness, may I not overlook Your Spirit who gently brings me the refreshing "dew from heaven." Amen.

THE SPIRIT OF THE LORD

Should it be said, O house of Jacob: "Is the Spirit of the Lord angry? Does he do such things?" (Micah 2:7)

These words were spoken by false prophets in the face of Micah's prediction of coming judgment. He warned Judah that because of persistent idolatry the nation would be overrun by an enemy army. God had seen the extortion, the greed, the oppression of the poor; now He was about to act.

Oh no, said the false prophets. Is the Spirit of God angry? Would He do such things? They assumed the answer was no. But they were wrong. The Spirit of God *was* angry. He *would* do such things.

Many people—even many Christian people—persist in a false notion of God. They fervently hope and pray that God's anger is just a myth, a fable promulgated by cranky preachers to keep their congregations in line.

But God's anger burns against sin. He will not stand idly by while His people who bear His name disobey His commandments.

In the years to come, the false prophets found out the hard way that Micah was right: God's Spirit was indeed angry. Sometimes we need to remember that deliberate disobedience requires stern discipline. Parents who love their children react quickly when they see their own flesh and blood acting foolishly.

As Hebrews 12 reminds us, discipline some-times seem harsh but it yields a great harvest of righteousness (v. 11). If we say to the Lord, "Make me feel good," we will miss a large part of what He is saying to us.

Because God loves us, He won't let His children get away with sin forever.

Will the Spirit of God ever be angry? Yes, in-deed. And we do well not to forget that fact.

Father, Your anger is but one side of Your great love. Thank You for caring enough not to let me go on in sin forever. Amen.

THE EYES OF THE LORD

These seven are the eyes of the Lord, which range throughout the earth. (Zechariah 4:10)

Eventually God gave Zechariah a series of visions, in part to encourage the rebuilding of the temple. In the fifth night vision (4:1–14), Zechariah saw a golden lampstand (the means of giving light in the temple) fed by a bowl of oil suspended above it. As oil continuously flowed from the bowl into the lampstand, the light continually shined in the darkness.

An angel explained the meaning to the perplexed Zechariah. The oil was a symbol of the Holy Spirit. As the people relied on the Holy Spirit and not on their own strength (v. 6), the temple would indeed be completed. Although rebuilding the temple seemed like moving a gigantic mountain (v. 7), with the help of the Spirit, the work would eventually be completed. When the capstone was finally in place, people would shout "God bless it! God bless it!" That is, the people would shout for joy, declaring that the temple had been built by God's grace alone.

Though the beginning is small and despised by the world, the ending will be a great victory for God (v. 10).

There were seven lights on the lampstand, signifying the "eyes of the Lord," which see things the eyes of man might miss. Do the people doubt that the temple will be rebuilt? Do they bemoan its small size compared with the vast glory of Solomon's temple? No matter, for the Lord sees that the work will indeed be completed.

Because the Holy Spirit is there, the work will be done. Thank God for the "eyes of the Lord" that see beyond all human limitation. Nothing is impossible with God.

The old gospel song says, "Little is much, if God is in it." Indeed it is so.

Father, teach me to see with the eyes of faith, believing that if You are in it, You will complete it. Amen.

SPIRIT OF GRACE AND SUPPLICATION

And I will pour out on the house of David and the inhabitants of Jerusalem a spirit of grace and supplication. (Zechariah 12:10)

When the Lord Jesus Christ returns to the earth, Israel will experience a great national turning to the Lord. Zechariah 12 describes how the Holy Spirit will be poured out on the nation, resulting in deep personal mourning as they "look on me, the one they have pierced." The promise is very specific in verse 10: it is for the "house of David" and the "inhabitants of Jerusalem." On that day when the spiritual blinders are removed, the people of Israel will realize the great folly that occurred at Jesus' first coming, when the rulers of the nation conspired together to crucify Him. On that day, they will see Jesus as if seeing Him for the very first time, they will weep for their own sins, they will mourn how badly He was mistreated. Verse 11 notes that "on that day the weeping in Jerusalem will be great"—as well it should be, for it was there that Jesus was crucified.

But the mourning leads to something so great that only God could imagine it: the national conversion of Israel. "On that day a fountain will be opened to the house of David and the inhabitants of Jerusalem, to cleanse them from sin and impurity" (13:1).

How will such a miracle take place? Zechariah 12:10 tells us that it begins when the Spirit of grace and supplication is poured out on the people. The Holy Spirit will minister grace to the people of Israel and lead them to deep repentance and cleansing for their sin. When that happens, the new covenant promised by the prophets will finally be fulfilled.

It is the same Spirit who today brings us into God's family. He is the one who causes us to mourn over our sin. He causes us to look to Jesus who was pierced for our transgressions. He is the one who leads us to Calvary's fountain where our sins are washed away. He gives us a new heart and a new desire to serve God. He awakens within us a love of God we never had before. He changes us so that where once we loved sin now we love to do what is right.

The most amazing fact is this: What God has done for believers today, He will someday do for Israel when Jesus returns to the earth. Herod will not have the last word. Jesus will someday reign over His own people from David's throne in Jerusalem.

We have God's promise on that, and the Holy Spirit will make it happen.

Father, the greatest moments of human history are all in Your hands. I say with the saints of all ages, "Even so, come, Lord Jesus." Amen.

WATER

On that day living water will flow out from Jerusalem, half to the eastern sea and half to the western sea, in summer and in winter.
(Zechariah 14:8)

Water is one of the most common symbols for the Holy Spirit in the Bible. Since water is indispensable for human life, the phrase "living water" is an apt metaphor for the Spirit's work in the human heart. Zechariah 14:8 looks forward to a time after the return of Christ when the climate and geography of earth will be changed as Jesus Christ sets up His kingdom on the earth. There will be a great earthquake, splitting the Mount of Olives in two (v. 4), followed by enormous changes in the normal pattern of daytime and nighttime (vv. 6–7). On that day "living water" will flow from Jerusalem. This is no doubt both literal and symbolic. There will be a literal river, but the river will symbolize the free flow of the Spirit throughout the entire earth.

Jesus used this word picture in John 4 during His conversation with the woman at the well. Although she came seeking literal water, He promised to give her "living water" which would satisfy her thirst forever (John 4:10). That "living water" becomes a "spring of water" within the heart of the believer, welling up to eternal life. As the water rises rapidly in the well, it comes to the surface and flows over the edges.

What a wonderful picture of how the Spirit works in the human heart. Those who come to Christ find "living water" that satisfies the deep thirst within. Through the indwelling Holy Spirit, that "living water" produces a new life that eventually bubbles to the surface and becomes evident to others. Living water won't become stagnant. It always produces a dynamic, abundant, exciting new life.

Water is also necessary for cleansing. Ephesians 5:26 pictures this aspect of the Spirit's work when it mentions the "washing with water through the Word." The Word is the cleansing agent; the Spirit is the cleansing power. As the Spirit applies the Word to our lives, we are cleansed from the stain of sin and the filth of the world.

The Holy Spirit flows through believers like a mighty river of living water, bringing new life and providing deep, inner cleansing. As we yield ourselves to Christ, the abundance of His life (the "living water") flows out to those around us.

River of God, I live in a dry, barren land. All around me men and women die of thirst. Make me a channel of living water to those who desperately need it. Amen.

THE DOVE

At that moment heaven was opened, and he saw the Spirit of God descending like a dove and lighting on him. (Matthew 3:16)

At Christ's baptism, the Holy Spirit descended upon Him "like a dove." The dove is a particularly appropriate symbol because it is a beautiful, graceful bird. In Matthew 10:16, Jesus told His disciples to be "as shrewd as snakes and as innocent as doves." The word dove implies a guileless, open-book, "what you see is what you get" heart attitude. Applied to the Holy Spirit, it means that the Spirit Himself is pure, open, and honest—and produces the same qualities in the people He touches. As the dove descended from heaven, even so the Holy Spirit comes down from heaven to bless the people of the earth. Note that the dove rested on Christ, symbolizing the peace that the Holy Spirit brings. The fact that the dove came directly to Christ shows also the personal relationship the Holy Spirit has with each believer. Finally, the dove resting on Christ demonstrates the Father's divine approval of the Son's mission on earth. Once the dove landed on Christ, the voice from heaven said: "This is My Son, whom I love; with Him I am well pleased" (Matthew 3:17). All three persons of the Trinity are thus represented at the baptism of Jesus.

This symbol of the Spirit has a great deal to say to us about the effect of the Holy Spirit on our lives. When the Holy Spirit comes: (1) He brings peace to our souls; (2) He comes quietly, without fanfare; (3) He establishes a personal relationship with us; (4) He produces gentleness within, not a harsh and critical spirit; (5) He leads us toward purity, honesty, and a truly "harmless" life; (6) He brings God's divine approval that we are indeed His children; (7) He leads us toward a beautiful, grace-filled Christian life.

Spirit of God, as You descended from heaven upon Jesus, descend on me today that I might know the fullness of Your power. Amen.

*For it will not be you speaking, but the Spirit of
your Father speaking through you.*
(Matthew 10:20)

In Matthew 10, Jesus told His followers several
important facts about the future: (1) they will face
harsh opposition in the world; (2) this opposition
will often come from religious people; (3) such
persecution will bring the followers of Christ before "governors and kings"; (4) Christ ordained
such things in order that His followers might have
an opportunity to explain their faith publicly;
(5) when that happens, believers should not fear
but should trust the Holy Spirit to tell them what to
say.

Such straight talk unnerves many Christians. After all, most of us would prefer to live a quiet life
with our family and friends. But Jesus warns us
that it won't always be so easy for some of us. "I
did not come to bring peace, but a sword" (v. 34).
Truth always cuts both ways. Sometimes living for
Christ brings us into direct opposition with the
rulers of this world.

What should we say when the school principal
calls us because our child attended a prayer meet-
ing at the flag pole? How do we respond when our
boss tells us not to read our Bible during our
lunch break? How does a Christian nurse respond
when instructed to assist in performing an abor-
tion? What about the pastor who is threatened

with losing his pension if he speaks out against gay rights in his own denomination? How does a godly wife answer the ridicule of her unbelieving husband every Sunday morning?

These are not easy questions, but they are real-life circumstances that the followers of Christ face every day. Being a Christian in a pagan society isn't going to win many popularity contests. Sooner or later someone will put us on the spot for what we believe. What do we do then?

The answer is, don't worry about it. In that moment of crisis, the Holy Spirit will show us what to say and do. Does that mean we shouldn't prepare ahead of time? No, but it *does* mean we shouldn't worry ahead of time. Those who are faithful to Christ can rest in the confidence that the Holy Spirit will be with them when their faith is under fire.

We don't need to go looking for trouble. If we are faithful to Christ, sooner or later, trouble will find us. Jesus said to be on guard, but don't be afraid.

If standing up for Jesus gets us in trouble, fear not, because the Holy Spirit will be standing up with us.

Father, thank You for sending Your Spirit to tell me what to say when trouble comes. May I never be ashamed of Jesus or afraid to speak up for Him. Amen.

Every sin and blasphemy will be forgiven men, but the blasphemy against the Spirit will not be forgiven. (Matthew 12:31)

These solemn words of Jesus warn of a sin so awesome that it can never be forgiven. For those who believe in the grace of God, this poses a perplexing problem: *How can any sin be so horrible that God will not forgive it?*

The context helps answer that question. Jesus had just healed a demon-possessed boy who was deaf and mute. All the people were astonished and wondered if Jesus was the promised Messiah. In order to stop such speculation, the Pharisees told the people that Jesus had done this miracle by the power of Beelzebub—that is, by the prince of demons.

This accusation reveals the monstrous evil inside the Pharisees. If they had said, "He's just another miracle-worker," that wouldn't have been as bad. If they had said, "He's just a fake," that would have been a terrible slam, but still not as bad. To accuse Christ of working miracles by the power of Beelzebub was to utterly reject His Messiahship and say that He was an agent of Satan. Not only were they turning the truth upside down, but they were at the same time cutting themselves off from their only hope of salvation.

Furthermore, the Pharisees *knew better.* This wasn't a half-baked comment of men who were mad because Jesus had upstaged them. It was a calculated, deliberate, premeditated attempt to destroy His ministry. Since the Pharisees represented the religious leadership of Israel, their rejection of Christ sealed His fate.

From that day forward, they hated Him with an ever-increasing hatred, culminating in the plot that led to His arrest and ultimately to His crucifixion.

In that time and place, at that crystallized moment of history, the Pharisees crossed a line they could never uncross. Their sin was unpardonable because it represented a decisive, national rejection of Jesus Christ as the Messiah of Israel. They blamed evil spirits for what had been done through the Holy Spirit.

Can the unpardonable sin be committed today? Not in the precise sense of Matthew 12 because the exact situation can never be duplicated. But the same hard-hearted attitude exists whenever sinners resist the Holy Spirit's call to repentance and faith in Christ.

Those who choose to resist the Spirit's work may eventually so harden themselves that they develop a seared conscience. In that case their sin is unpardonable precisely because they choose not to be pardoned. The door is locked from the inside.

Father, I pray for my friends who don't know Jesus. Grant them tender hearts to respond to the call of Your Spirit. Amen.

The angel answered, "The Holy Spirit will come upon you, and the power of the Most High will overshadow you." (Luke 1:35)

Across the centuries, the Virgin Birth of Jesus Christ has been considered a foundational doctrine by Christians of virtually every denomination. Both Matthew and Luke plainly ascribe the conception of Jesus Christ to the action of the Holy Spirit. Matthew uses phrases such as "through the Holy Spirit" and "from the Holy Spirit" to describe what happened. Luke adds an intriguing phrase when he reports the angel Gabriel's words to Mary: "The Holy Spirit will come upon you, and the power of the Most High will overshadow you" (Luke 1:35). The verb for "overshadow" speaks of the direct, personal presence of God. The same verb is used in all three accounts of the Transfiguration to describe the cloud that enveloped Jesus, Moses, and Elijah (and Peter, James, and John) on the mountain. From that cloud came a voice saying, "This is my Son," even as Gabriel told Mary, "The holy one to be born will be called the Son of God."

What is the significance of Jesus' being begotten of the Holy Spirit? Since Jesus was born of Mary, we know that He was truly human. Since He was conceived through the Holy Spirit, we know that He was more than a man.

The Virgin Birth was God's way of announcing to the world that Jesus was indeed His Son. We'll never know if God could have done it some other way, because He did it *this way*. The unique entrance of the Son of God into the world proves that Jesus was indeed "the Word made flesh" (John 1:14). Through the Virgin Birth, the Son of God entered the human race, taking upon Himself all aspects of true humanity, yet remaining sinless, and without surrendering any aspect of His deity.

Thus the babe in the manger was truly Almighty God from heaven. He was fully God and yet fully man at the same time. Deity and humanity joined together. Theologians use a big word to describe Jesus. They call Him the theanthropic person (the God-Man).

What role did the Holy Spirit play? Through some means unknown to us, during the "overshadowing" He created within the womb of Mary the unborn (yet fully human and fully alive) Person of Jesus Christ.

As so often throughout the Bible, the Holy Spirit is not the center of attention. Yet He is always there, acting as the "agent" of the Father's will. He is the One who creates the human life of the Son of God.

It is a pure miracle of the highest order. No one can explain it or duplicate it. The Virgin Birth of Jesus stands absolutely alone. Nothing can be compared to it because no other birth has been—or ever could be—like it.

It is a truth to be believed. A fundamental fact to be accepted. A miracle at which to marvel. An amazing beginning for the God-Man. It was a birth like no other because Jesus was indeed God's one and only Son.

Father, I believe in the Virgin Birth because I believe Your Word. As I contemplate this miracle, increase my faith to believe that nothing is impossible with You. Amen.

And the power of the Lord was present for him to heal the sick. (Luke 5:17)

Luke 5:17–26 contains the famous story of the man who was lowered through the roof so that Jesus could heal him. It teaches many lessons regarding persistence, the power of faith, and Jesus' true identity.

Verse 17 sets the scene for us. One day as Jesus was teaching in Capernaum, the crowds were so great that no one could get in the door. They had come to hear this amazing rabbi from Nazareth. He taught truths about God that the Pharisees had somehow overlooked. When He spoke, He used vivid word pictures, illustrations from nature, and stories from everyday life. Unlike some of the learned rabbis, Jesus felt no need to impress anyone with His great intellect. He had come to bring people nearer to God, so He had no need to impress anyone.

But they came for more than the teaching. Jesus had the power to work miracles. No one—not even His enemies—could deny that fact. He healed the sick, caused the blind to see and the deaf to hear, and cast out demons. He even raised the dead.

No wonder they flocked to Him.

Luke tells us that "the power of the Lord was present for Him to heal the sick." That phrase takes us back to Jesus' conception when "the Power of the Most High" overshadowed Mary. Luke 4:14 tells us that Jesus returned to Galilee from His temptation "in the power of the Spirit." The people of Capernaum were amazed at His power over demons: "What is this teaching? With authority and power He gives orders to evil spirits and they come out!" (Luke 4:36).

The power of Jesus and the power of the Holy Spirit are one and the same. God is the source of power over sickness, demonic spirits, and death. The Father gave the Son the power of the Spirit that He might work His mighty miracles.

There are three important lessons here. First, the Holy Spirit is God's divine channel for releasing His power on the earth. Second, when God's power is released into any situation, no power on earth can stand against it. Third, as we depend on the Holy Spirit, we will discover that God's power is available to us in every situation.

God never asks us to face our problems alone. Through the Holy Spirit, we have access to the greatest power source in the universe.

The power we need is ours for the asking.

Gracious Father, when will I learn the folly of facing my problems alone? Thank You for providing Your Spirit to help me live victoriously. Amen.

THE FINGER OF GOD

*But if I drive out demons by the finger of God,
then the kingdom of God has come to you.*
(Luke 11:20)

This particular symbol for the Holy Spirit comes
from Exodus 8:19, where Pharaoh's magicians correctly surmised that the plagues had come to Egypt
as a result of "the finger of God." Exodus 31:18
tells us that the Ten Commandments were given
to Moses on two tablets inscribed by the "finger of
God." Psalm 8:3 adds the important fact that the
heavens are "the work of your fingers."

When the Pharisees accused Jesus of casting
out demons by the power of Beelzebub (that is, by
the power of Satan himself), Jesus replied that
their accusations were both illogical and incon-
sistent. It was illogical to suggest that Satan would
cast out demons by his own power because he
would then be opposing himself. Furthermore,
since Jewish exorcists regularly claimed to cast
out demons, to accuse Jesus was to accuse their
own followers as well. They would rise up in judgment against the Pharisees for suggesting such a
thing (v. 19).

Only one conclusion can be drawn from the
miracles performed by Jesus: "The kingdom of
God has come to you" (v. 20). For thousands of
years Satan had ruled the earth—not as its rightful
owner, but as a usurper. In a sense, the whole story
of the Bible is the story of God moving to reclaim

that which is rightfully His. Though the world belonged to Him by creation, it had fallen into evil hands. Now the King Himself had come to stake His claim on the earth.

Since the days of Jesus, Satan has been a defeated foe. Though he continues to fight against the Lord, his doom is sure, his final destiny in the lake of fire guaranteed by the victory Christ won at the cross.

The kingdom of God truly came in the person of Jesus the King. One day not long from now He will return once again to establish His kingdom on the earth.

Today, Satan is doing all he can to destroy God's work in the world. That includes attacking and harassing the people of God and tempting them to sin. But those who follow Christ closely will discover that Jesus is stronger than Satan.

He won the battle two thousand years ago. He is still the victor today.

Lord Jesus, I lift up Your name for You have triumphed over Satan and all his evil forces. I praise You for allowing me to share in Your great victory. Amen.

CLOTHING

I am going to send you what my Father has promised; but stay in the city until you have been clothed with power from on high.
(Luke 24:49)

Jesus spoke these words when He appeared to His disciples late on Easter Sunday. At first they were frightened because they thought He was a ghost (Luke 24:37–39). In order to prove He had really risen from the dead, He ate a piece of broiled fish in their presence (vv. 40–43). Affirming that everything that had happened to Him was in accordance with the Scriptures, He commissioned the disciples to preach the Gospel to all nations, beginning in Jerusalem (vv. 44–47). They were to declare to others what they themselves had witnessed (v. 48).

But they were not to begin until the promised Holy Spirit had been poured out on them—which took place fifty days later at Pentecost. At that time they would be "clothed with power from on high" (v. 49).

The phrase "clothed with power" describes the effect the coming of the Holy Spirit would have on them. In the first place, clothing covers human weakness. No more would the disciples have to depend on their own power; now they would be "covered" by the Holy Spirit. Second, clothing identifies the wearer. Football players wear uniforms, as do soldiers and sailors. Christ promised

His disciples that they would soon have a new "uniform"—the power of the Holy Spirit. Third, clothing in the Bible often identifies a person as a divine representative. Just as the priests in the Old Testament had special vestments to wear that set them apart from other people, even so the disciples would now "wear" the Holy Spirit as the mark of their relationship with God.

Most importantly, the disciples were not told to "clothe themselves" with the Holy Spirit. Instead, God Himself would clothe the disciples with the power of the Spirit. No one can "put on" the Holy Spirit, nor are we ever commanded to do so. That is solely the work of God on our behalf.

Clothing takes up a large part of our lives. We spend money and time to find just the right shirt, skirt, blouse, or tie. Many people have an entire closet filled with clothes for every occasion. We care about our clothing because, as the saying goes, "clothes make the man."

What does the well-dressed Christian wear? The answer is, the Holy Spirit. The very moment we come to Christ, the Holy Spirit gives us a brand-new wardrobe. We exchange the tattered rags of filthy self-righteousness for the dazzling garments of a brand-new life. For hatred we receive love. For misery, joy. For bitterness, forgiveness. For cowardice, boldness. For stinginess, compassion. For pride, humility. For envy, contentment.

What happens to those "rags" of the old life? God throws them away. We don't have to wear them any more unless we go dig them out of the trash. And why would we? Through the Holy Spirit, God clothes us with the beauty of Jesus Christ.

To this we should add that the distinctive mark of the Christian is not some special outward dress. Those things don't matter one way or the other. What matters is that we "wear" the Holy Spirit in all our daily relationships.

No one is more beautiful than a Christian who is dressed in the Holy Spirit.

Spirit of God, may the beauty of Jesus be seen in me today. Amen.

The wind blows wherever it pleases. You hear its sound, but you cannot tell where it comes from or where it is going. So it is with everyone born of the Spirit. (John 3:8)

Wind serves as a particularly good symbol of the Holy Spirit. As Jesus points out to Nicodemus, wind by its very nature is invisible and unpredictable. The wind that blows today from the north may blow from the south tomorrow or from the east or west or not at all. We feel its effect and hear it whistling through the leaves, but the wind itself is totally free from man's control. Wind exists everywhere on the earth, is continually in motion, and may be experienced in varying degrees —from a slight breeze to a mighty rushing wind to the destructive force of a tornado.

In a closed room, the air soon becomes stagnant. But when the window is open, the incoming wind blows out the stifling air. On a hot summer's day, a cool breeze refreshes everyone.

In John 20:22, Jesus breathed on His disciples and said, "Receive the Holy Spirit." On the day of Pentecost in Acts 2:2, the Holy Spirit came with the sound like "the blowing of a violent wind." Just as the wind filled the whole house where they were sitting, the disciples themselves were all filled with the Holy Spirit.

Peter uses the imagery of a driving wind to picture the writers of Scripture being carried along by the Holy Spirit (2 Peter 1:21). As the wind moves a ship's sails, so the Holy Spirit moved the prophets so that what they said was exactly what God wanted.

Just as the wind is everywhere in the world, even so the Holy Spirit's work is universal, not limited to one country, region, or race of humanity. Similar to the unpredictability of the wind, no one can say for certain where the Spirit will blow in great power today or tomorrow. As the wind is beyond man's control, in the same way no one can control the work of the Spirit. As the wind blows from the heavens, so the Holy Spirit is sent from heaven.

This symbol of the Holy Spirit as God's wind ought to greatly encourage us. How we need the fresh wind of the Spirit today! He alone can wake us out of our spiritual lethargy. He alone can dispel the toxic fumes of unbelief and carnality. He alone can bring the sweet aroma of heaven back into our lives.

O Wind of God, blow upon me today. Amen.

THE SPIRIT GIVEN WITHOUT LIMIT

For the one whom God has sent speaks the words of God, for God gives the Spirit without limit. (John 3:34)

This section of John's Gospel repeatedly stresses the superiority of Jesus to John the Baptist. Although John the Baptist was significant in his own right, he could never be compared to Jesus. For one thing, John himself said, "He must become greater; I must become less" (v. 30). John explains what he means in the following verses:

- Jesus is from heaven; John is from earth (v. 31).
- Jesus speaks with divine authority (vv. 32–33).
- Jesus speaks the words of God (v. 34a).
- Jesus has been given the Spirit without limit (v. 34b).
- The Father has placed everything in Jesus' hands (v. 35).
- Jesus is the source of eternal life to those who believe in Him (v. 36).

These astounding claims could never be made about any mere man, but only about the Son of God. It is in that context that we must examine the truth that Jesus was given the Spirit "without limit." This phrase is evidently meant to contrast Jesus with the prophets of the Old Testament (of which John the Baptist would be a typical example). As we have already discovered, the Holy Spirit in the

Old Testament was given to believers temporarily and selectively. This explains why the Spirit could be said to suddenly "come upon" one of the prophets or Samson more than once. Though the Holy Spirit was very active in the Old Testament, He evidently did not permanently indwell believers during that period.

By contrast, Jesus was given the full measure of the Spirit's power. As the God-Man, He had the full resources of the Holy Spirit available to Him at all times and in all situations, without any human impediment (such as sin) standing in the way. Such a statement could never be made about anyone before Christ, nor could it be made in precisely the same sense of anyone today.

Even today, believers contend with human impediments (such as the pull of our sinful flesh) that hinder to one degree or another the Spirit's work in our lives. Nevertheless, as we yield ourselves continually to the Lord and depend upon the power of the Spirit, we will discover an increasing reality of His divine work in us.

No—it will never be precisely the same for us as it was for Christ. No one can or should make such a claim. Yet through the cross a significant victory has been won. Because Christ died and rose again, we now experience new life (Romans 6). As we yield our bodies to God, the human impediments are lessened and we experience more of the Holy Spirit's divine power at work in us.

So there are two things we should take away from this truth about "the Spirit given without limit": (1) Christ is indeed superior to all human leaders, no matter how good or great they may be; (2) as we yield ourselves to God, we discover more and more of the Spirit's power, which Jesus experienced without limit 100 percent of the time.

Following Jesus leads us into a deeper experience of the Holy Spirit's power.

Father, please make me like Christ so that I might discover more of the Spirit's power in my daily life. Amen.

Whoever believes in me, as the Scripture has said, streams of living water will flow from within him. (John 7:38)

These dramatic words came from the lips of Jesus as He spoke to a vast crowd gathered in Jerusalem for the last and greatest day of the Feast of Tabernacles. As the assembled multitudes strained to hear His words—some curious, others skeptical, still others moved by a deep inner need—Jesus offered them something that only God could provide—"streams of living water" that would flow from within them out to the world around them.

Lest anyone misunderstand His words, John tells us in verse 39 that "he meant the Spirit." In short, Jesus was offering something brand new in the history of the world, a complete inner transformation by means of the Holy Spirit.

Jesus' words must have shocked His hearers with their stunning simplicity: "If anyone is thirsty, let him come to me and drink." (v. 37) That short statement contains the essence of the Gospel message. It is centered in a person—Jesus Christ. It is offered to all without restriction—If *anyone.* It is predicated upon human need—If anyone is *thirsty.* It demands a personal response—Let Him *come to me.* It invites personal participation—and *drink.*

Those who respond to the call receive the Holy Spirit as a permanent, indwelling, life-changing presence. To speak of "streams of living water" highlights four facts about the Spirit's ministry in the believer:

- He takes up residence within the "inner being."
- He "flows" with an inexhaustible supply.
- He brings the life of God to the soul.
- He satisfies the deep thirst inside every heart.

Finally, this word picture also seems to imply a "flowing out" from inside the believer to the lives of those around him. As the "living water" flows from within, other thirsty people will wonder, "He used to be thirsty just like me. Where did all that water come from?"

If we are dying in the desert, the most important thing in the world is a cup of cold water. Jesus promises more than a cup. He promises a never-ending flow of clear, cool, clean living water. Streams without pollution. Rivers that will never run dry.

That's what the Holy Spirit provides for you. He will fill your life with living water. If you are thirsty, take a drink and see for yourself.

Lord, may the streams of living water flow through me so that others may be thirsty to know You. Amen.

*And I will ask the Father, and he will give you
another Counselor to be with you forever.*
(John 14:16)

Among all the names of the Holy Spirit, none is so
well known as the name "Counselor." Many Christians
also know the Greek word that it translates—
parakletos. The King James Version translates it
as "Comforter." Other suggestions are "Helper" or
"Advocate." The word itself means "one who is
called alongside to help." It has within it the idea
of coming to the aid of someone in need and doing
for that person what he cannot do for himself.
Thus a lawyer becomes an advocate for the accused,
a doctor rushes to the aid of her patients, a
coach instructs his players, a mother consoles her
children, a captain rescues his soldiers, a professor
tutors her failing students, and so on.

Someone has said that "Counselor" or "Helper"
is Christ's favorite title for the Holy Spirit. No doubt
that is true, since almost every occurrence comes
from our Lord's Upper Room Discourse, John 13–
17. That fact takes on extra significance when we
note that Jesus spoke these words just a few hours
before His crucifixion. In those dark hours, as
wicked men schemed to take His life, knowing
that all too soon He would be taken from His disciples,
Jesus gave His men a word of encouragement
regarding the things that were about to
happen.

If we summarized the message, it might sound like this: "Men, sooner than you think I will be taken from you. But do not fear. After I am gone, I will send the Holy Spirit who will take my place. He will be with you wherever you go. When the time comes, He will bring to your mind all the things I have taught you. He will also convict the world of its sin and will teach believers the truth of God. You'll have some difficult times, but the Holy Spirit will be a Counselor, a Guide, an Advocate, and a Friend. He will help you in every situation you face. I know that you'll miss me, but that is why I am sending the Spirit. He will take my place and through Him, you will accomplish even greater works than I have done."

The words of Jesus must have been a great comfort to the disciples. But I imagine that they meant much more six months later than they did that night. As long as Jesus was physically present, the promise of the Spirit didn't mean a great deal. Only after His departure did they realize what a great gift Christ had given them.

The word "Counselor" implies two things: someone is in trouble, and someone else is coming to the rescue. Without trouble, no one needs a "Counselor" or a "Helper" or a "Comforter."

Where do you turn when you are in trouble? To a husband or wife? But single people don't have that option. To a friend? But friends aren't always available. To your children or your parents? But they won't always be there. To your church? But no church can be there all the time in every situation. To some outside agency? But you may have to wait six months to get an appointment.

"If only Jesus were here," you think, "He would help me out." Jesus isn't here physically, and if He were, He could only be in one place at one time. That's why He promised to send the Holy Spirit.

He knew that sooner or later, we'd all be in trouble. He knew that sooner or later, all human friends and loved ones would fail us. He knew that if He didn't do something, none of us would make it.

So He sent the Holy Spirit in His place. No one is an orphan, no one is ever left alone.

All of God's children have at least one Friend, one Helper, one Counselor, one Comforter. Chew on that thought for a moment. We are not alone. Jesus made sure of that.

You may think you are alone. You may feel that way right now, and circumstances may even point to that conclusion. But you aren't alone. The Holy Spirit is with you to help you in your distress.

Believe it. We have the word of Jesus on it. We are not alone.

Thank You, Lord Jesus, for remembering how weak I am. I praise You for the gift of the Holy Spirit, my Counselor, Helper, Comforter, and Friend. Amen.

SPIRIT OF TRUTH

. . .the Spirit of truth. The world cannot accept him, because it neither sees him nor knows him. (John 14:17)

Here is a title pregnant with meaning. To call the Holy Spirit the "Spirit of truth" is to say that His very essence and character is grounded in the Truth. The Holy Spirit speaks only the truth about the Father, the Son, God's will, sin, and salvation.

There are other spirits in the world—evil spirits, lying spirits, spirits of confusion and deception. These spirits (which are really demons) mislead many people by masquerading as the Spirit of God. In 1 John 4:1–4, we find a very practical way to "test the spirits." We are instructed to ask them what they believe about Jesus Christ. Is He really the Son of God? Is He really "the Word made flesh"? Do they believe in the Incarnation? If the answers are no, or if the spirits equivocate, they are not the Spirit of truth. What the Holy Spirit says and does is always in perfect accordance with the Word of God.

For that matter, if someone comes to us and claims to have a revelation from God, but the revelation contains falsehoods or untruths of any kind, we can reject it immediately. It did not come from the Spirit of truth.

There is another fascinating side of this name. Jesus said that "the world cannot accept Him" because the world neither sees nor knows Him. The

Holy Spirit does not operate on the world's wave-length. That is why many try so hard to explain away the Christian faith. The world doesn't know God the Father, Jesus Christ, or the Holy Spirit! Perhaps that also gives an insight into the strange mysticism of these days. When men turn away from God's truth, they will believe any lie—rein-carnation, voodoo, spiritualism, or warmed-over, "all religions are basically the same" propaganda. The Holy Spirit is not involved in any of those un-truths. He is the Spirit of truth who teaches no error.

Strange things are often done and said in the name of the Holy Spirit. Yet the Spirit of truth nev-er leads anyone to say or do anything that is con-trary to the Word of God. God does not contradict Himself. His Word is truth, the Holy Spirit is the Spirit of truth. These two must always be held together.

One other emphasis should be noted. Since in John's Gospel, truth is always wrapped up in Je-sus Christ, the name "Spirit of truth" points to the Holy Spirit's role in bearing witness to Jesus. John 16:14 explicitly tells us that the Spirit will bring glory to Christ, not to Himself.

The Spirit of truth points people to Jesus. Those who follow the Spirit's leading will do the same thing. We won't just argue doctrine or answer hard questions. When the Spirit fills a believer, that person will bear witness to Jesus.

Spirit of truth, ground me in the Word of truth that I may bear witness to Jesus Christ who is the Truth. Amen.

THE SPIRIT WHO GOES
OUT FROM THE FATHER

*When the Counselor comes, whom I will send
to you from the Father, the Spirit of truth who
goes out from the Father, he will testify about
me.* (John 15:26)

This verse is the primary biblical basis for the doctrine called the procession of the Holy Spirit. During the Middle Ages theologians argued about whether the Holy Spirit proceeded from the Father alone, or from the Father *and* the Son. Various statements by Jesus in the Upper Room Discourse seem to imply the latter. Although the Spirit is "sent" by the Father, several times Jesus says that He will send the Spirit as well (John 15:26, 16:7).

Though the Spirit is "sent" by the Father and the Son, this does not diminish His essential deity and full equality with the Father and the Son. He is "sent" by the Father to do the Father's work on earth, and He is "sent" by the Son to be "another Counselor" in the place of Jesus Christ.

There is never any hint of jealousy within the Trinity. What the Spirit does always meets with the full approval of the Father and the Son. To be filled with the Spirit is to be filled with God and with the Spirit of Christ.

While we wait for the return of Christ, the only daily experience we have with God is our experience with His Spirit. But since the Spirit is "sent" by the Father and the Son, to know the Holy Spirit is truly to know the Father and the Son, as much as anyone can know God given the limitations of human flesh. Though sent by the Father and the Son, the Holy Spirit is not less than God, but is Himself fully God.

These are vast mysteries, which no mortal will ever comprehend. Let us content ourselves with this thought: To know the Holy Spirit is to know God as much as anyone ever can.

Holy Spirit, please make the things of God real to me today. Amen.

FIRE

They saw what seemed to be tongues of fire that separated and came to rest on each of them. (Acts 2:3)

Fire is one of the most frequent biblical images for God's presence with His people. The connection is made in such passages as Exodus 3:1–5 (Moses and the burning bush); Exodus 13:21 (the pillar of fire); Leviticus 9:24 (fire from the Lord consuming the burnt offering); 1 Kings 18:24 ("The god who answers by fire—he is God."); Isaiah 6:1–8 (coals of fire from the altar in heaven); Matthew 3:11 ("He will baptize you with the Holy Spirit and with fire."); Acts 2:3 ("They saw what seemed to be tongues of fire."); 1 Thessalonians 5:19 ("Do not put out the Spirit's fire."); and Hebrews 12:29 ("for our 'God is a consuming fire.'").

God sent the "tongues of fire" on the day of Pentecost as a sign that He was about to pour out the Holy Spirit in a new and powerful way. Just as the fiery pillar represented God's personal presence with His people, the Holy Spirit takes up residence in all believers. But now God's presence will be personal and individual—thus the "tongues of fire" rested on each person individually. Whereas God's presence came to the nation as a whole in the Old Testament, today each believer has the great privilege of having the personal presence of God through the indwelling of the Holy Spirit. And just as the fiery pillar gave clear direction outwardly, even so the Holy Spirit gives each believer inward direction. This represents a tremendous advance in God's program for His people. Where once He worked primarily in and through a *nation*, now He works in and through *individuals*.

In reference to the Holy Spirit, fire represents:

- God's presence with His people.
- God's protection of His people.
- God's cleansing of His people.
- God's judgment of His people.
- God's divine enablement of His people.
- God's gracious activity in the assembly of His people.

Some applications quickly suggest themselves from this theme. First, the Holy Spirit is God's divine cleansing agent, burning away the dross of sin and purifying us for service. Second, when we yield ourselves to the Holy Spirit, He fills us with the fire of God's presence. Third, during times of revival, the Holy Spirit spreads like a flame, igniting families, churches, communities, and entire nations. Finally, the Holy Spirit is the "fire" we need to let our light shine brightly for Jesus Christ.

O Flame of God, set me on fire with holy zeal. Ignite my heart with holy passion. Amen.

Exalted to the right hand of God, he has received from the Father the promised Holy Spirit and has poured out what you now see and hear. (Acts 2:33)

In Peter's powerful sermon on the day of Pentecost, he declared that Jesus had not only been raised from the dead (Acts 2:24–32), but that He had been exalted to the right hand of God—the highest position of honor in the universe. Because of His exaltation, God "gave" the Spirit to Jesus, who now poured out the Spirit on the disciples, resulting in "what you see and hear." That last phrase refers to the miracle whereby the disciples (who were relatively uneducated) spoke fluently in many foreign languages, enabling the Jews from every part of the Roman empire to hear the good news in their native tongues.

In essence, Peter based his argument on the Trinity, though he didn't use that word. The Father gave the Son permission to pour out the Spirit on the disciples. Peter mentioned the Holy Spirit in passing, simply to explain the miraculous events of Pentecost. But that wasn't the main point.

The real issue was that Peter was preaching to the very people who fifty-two days earlier had crucified Jesus. No doubt some of the mockers who laughed at Jesus hanging on the cross heard Peter's sermon. No laughter now. No more jeers. Too many unexplained things had happened—

not the least of which was the disappearance of Jesus' body.

Could it be that He had risen from the dead? If so, they had made a terrible mistake. Peter says as much as he drives home the truth: "Therefore let all Israel be assured of this: God has made this Jesus, whom you crucified, both Lord and Christ" (Acts 2:36).

They killed Him, but God raised Him from the dead. They thought they were rid of Him, but now He is exalted at the right hand of God. They thought it was all over, but now the Holy Spirit is working miracles before their very eyes.

No wonder they were "cut to the heart" (v. 37). Biblical preaching always does that.

Note that Peter referred to "the promised Holy Spirit." The reference goes back to the words of Jesus in Acts 1:4–8, and even farther back to the prophecy of John the Baptist in Mark 1:8. Ultimately it stretches back hundreds of years to the new covenant God promised Israel in Jeremiah 31:31–34. Isaiah, Ezekiel, and Joel also spoke of a time when the Holy Spirit would be poured out universally and permanently. When that happened, there would be deep inner transformation (Isaiah, Jeremiah, and Ezekiel) and also widespread outward evidence (Joel). Peter even quoted Joel 2:28–32, saying "This is what was spoken by the prophet Joel" (Acts 2:16).

What it means is, "God promised to send His Spirit, and now He has done it." Before the time of

Christ, the Holy Spirit came only to selected individuals who were chosen by God for some particular purpose.

Think of it! We now live in the age of the Spirit. What the prophets saw from a distance is the daily privilege of the Christian believer. No average Israelite ever knew the Holy Spirit the way we can. If we had lived in Jeremiah's day, his prophecy would have seemed too impossible to be believed. The same is true for those who heard Ezekiel speak of a "new heart and a new spirit." Even the people who heard Jesus in person didn't have the blessing of the "promised Holy Spirit" until the day of Pentecost.

What was promised has now arrived. What the ancients looked for has been our heritage for two thousand years.

Is it possible that we have taken the Holy Spirit for granted? Has our spiritual bounty made us ungrateful to God?

The great good news is this—Pentecost is past. The Holy Spirit has come. Let the people of God rejoice.

Father, when I am ungrateful, remind me what life would be like without Your Spirit. Amen.

THE GIFT

You will receive the gift of the Holy Spirit.
(Acts 2:38)

When Peter reached the climax of his sermon at Pentecost, so great was the effect that his audience interrupted Him (v. 37). What should they do in light of who Jesus is and the terrible mistake they had made in crucifying Him?

Some mistakes can be rectified; others cannot. Their sin could never be undone. The crucifixion would stand forever as a symbol of humanity's worst moment. No other crime would reach the same depth of evil because no one else would do what they had done—put the Son of God to death.

But there were two things Peter's audience needed to do (v. 38). First, they needed to repent. The word "repent" means to change the mind. Here, it involved a radical admission of their guilt regarding the death of Jesus. They needed to admit that Jesus was right and they were wrong. They needed to acknowledge the enormity of their crime against God. Nothing less would suffice. No excuses would be accepted.

Second, Peter's audience needed to be baptized. Baptism in our culture often involves little more than a religious ritual whereby we agree to get wet as the price of church membership. But in the first century, baptism marked the moment at which a person "crossed the line" between darkness and light, hell and heaven, the kingdom of Satan and the kingdom of God, the world and the church. Baptism was a public pledge of allegiance to Jesus Christ and to His church.

Peter was calling for a public declaration from his audience not only of their moral guilt but also of their new commitment to Jesus, the man they had recently crucified. He didn't mean to make it easy. It's almost as if he made it as hard as he could. Only the truly committed would respond to such a call.

But those who did respond would receive two great benefits. First, all their sins would be forgiven. But especially the greatest sin of all—their complicity in the murder of Jesus Christ. No greater sin could be imagined; no greater forgiveness could be offered. But that is exactly what Peter said. One of the Puritans wrote a book titled *Grace Abounding to the Chief of Sinners.* Peter's hearers must have felt something like that upon hearing that they could be forgiven.

Second, Peter promised them "the gift of the Holy Spirit." Remember, these people had just witnessed great miracles performed by the disciples through "the promised Holy Spirit." Those signs signified that the age of the Spirit had now begun. The outpouring of the Holy Spirit on the disciples was the real miracle of Pentecost, not the wind and the fire and the speaking in tongues. Those things were secondary; they served as signposts alerting the world that God was pouring out His

Spirit on everyone who believes in Jesus—young and old, man and woman, rich and poor, master and servant.

Best of all, the Holy Spirit is now being given as a gift. We don't have to agonize all night to receive the Spirit. He comes gift-wrapped from God the Father as one of the benefits of believing in Jesus.

Like salvation itself, we can't "earn" the Spirit by doing good works. He is the gift of God to every Christian.

Thus we see the great miracle of Pentecost. It represents the coming of the Holy Spirit upon all Christians without distinction. Remember, the miracles aren't the point; they simply alert us to the fact that something very significant is happening.

Where once the Spirit came and went, indwelling selected individuals for brief periods of time, He now comes to take up permanent residence in the heart of all believers all the time. This is the "promise" God fulfilled and "the gift" He gave at Pentecost.

Father, thank You for freeing me from the impossible burden of attempting to "earn" the Holy Spirit. With a grateful heart I receive Your gift to me. Amen.

You have lied to the Holy Spirit. (Acts 5:3)

You have not lied to men but to God. (Acts 5:4)

These two verses clearly refer to the Holy Spirit as God. They both come from Peter as he spoke to Ananias about his wicked deception. In those days, the early Christians voluntarily shared all their possessions (Acts 4:32–36). As a sign of his commitment, an early convert named Barnabas sold a field he owned and laid the money at the apostles' feet (v. 36).

Upon seeing that demonstration of godly commitment, Ananias determined to do the same thing —but with one crucial difference. He and his wife Sapphira had sold some property but agreed together to hold back part of the money and offer the remainder to the apostles (Acts 5:1–2).

Peter, having been informed by God of the couple's actions, confronted Ananias with his sin. The evil was not just the lying or withholding a part rather than offering the total dollars made. Ananias' sin involved a public deception—he pretended to give everything when he was really only giving a portion. He didn't have to sell the land in the first place, and he didn't have to bring the money to the apostles. The land and the money were always within his control.

God doesn't want our money; He wants our hearts. He certainly doesn't want a big public show of our commitment, especially when the commitment isn't backed up by our lives.

But with God, we always reap what we sow. Instead of being filled with the Holy Spirit, Ananias had allowed himself to be filled with Satan's power (v. 3). Thus he had lied to the Holy Spirit, which is the same as lying to God.

When he heard the words of Peter, Ananias fell over dead, right in the middle of the church service. Young men came forward, dragged his corpse outside, and buried him (vv. 5–6). Later, the same thing happened to his wife Sapphira (vv. 7–10). As word spread of God's harsh judgment, great fear seized the whole church and everyone who heard about these amazing events (v. 11).

Several applications can be drawn from this shocking story. First, the Holy Spirit is indeed God and must be accorded the same reverence given to the Father and to the Son. Second, when we turn away from the Holy Spirit's leading, we open ourselves to Satan's influence. Third, God will not be mocked. We must beware the sin of pretended commitment.

Lord God, let the searchlight of Your truth penetrate the hidden places within me. May what I say be backed up by the way I live. Amen.

*When they came to the border of Mysia, they
tried to enter Bithynia, but the Spirit of Jesus
would not allow them to.* (Acts 16:7)

Acts 16:6–10 contains several mysteries and much
useful information concerning God's will. The mysteries revolve around two divine refusals experienced by the apostle Paul and his company. At
two definite points early in his second missionary
journey, God specifically redirected his steps.

The first refusal came as Paul attempted to enter the province of Asia, due west of Lystra and
Derbe. But he was forbidden by the Holy Spirit to
go west (v. 6). So he and his companions headed
north, passing along the border between Galatia
and Phrygia. What happened? How did the Holy
Spirit "forbid" Paul to go to Asia? The answer is
that no one knows. It might have been through a
dream or by means of a voice from God or perhaps
by the word of a prophet. It's also possible that
certain natural circumstances—a washed-out road,
military disturbances, etc.—led Paul to conclude
that the Holy Spirit was directly blocking his way.

So Paul and his companions moved north, always intent on preaching the Gospel wherever they
went. As they moved beyond Galatia, they attempted to go east into Bithynia. Again they were refused, this time by the "Spirit of Jesus." Once again,
we are left to wonder exactly what is meant by this
phrase. Evidently the "Spirit of Jesus" and the "Holy

Spirit" were used interchangeably by Luke. If there is a difference, perhaps Paul received a vision of the risen Christ speaking directly to him, much like the one that took place on the Damascus road (Acts 9:4–6). But it is perfectly appropriate to refer to the Holy Spirit this way since the Lord Jesus sent Him to take His place.

Having been twice refused entrance into a particular province by the Spirit of the Lord, Paul's group now turned west, arriving at the port city of Troas. While there, Paul received a vision of the man from Macedonia (in Greece) saying, "Come over to Macedonia and help us" (Acts 16:9). Verse 10 ties it all together with this crucial comment: "After Paul had seen the vision, we got ready at once to leave for Macedonia, concluding that God had called us to preach the Gospel to them." The word translated "concluding" means to use all the facts at our disposal to arrive at a settled conclusion. It means that Paul and his associates carefully noted how the Holy Spirit had directed them step by step exactly where He wanted them to be. Then came the miraculous vision of the man from Macedonia.

It all fit. God wanted Paul to preach the Gospel in Greece. But that meant crossing the Aegean Sea. It also meant taking the Gospel from one continent to another, which represented a major westward shift in the expansion of Christianity.

All of us struggle with knowing God's will sooner or later. Should I take the new job or stay with the one I have? Should I get married? If so, who's going to be the lucky person? Does God want me on the mission field? Should we move to Greenville or to Portland, or should we stay in Chicago? The questions are endless.

This paragraph offers a useful guide to discovering God's will in the nitty-gritty of life. First, we need to make sure we are obeying God in what He wants us to do right now. Second, we must be flexible in light of changing circumstances. Third, we are to ask God to give us specific directions through whatever means He chooses. Fourth, we can trust the Holy Spirit to make God's will known to us at just the right time. Finally, we are to use all the information at our disposal to make wise decisions.

Will this remove all doubt? No. In this life most of our decisions will be tinged with some doubt. But we must ask ourselves, whose responsibility is it—ours or God's? The answer is, God takes responsibility to show us His will. Our part is to obey, to take one step of faith at a time, and to follow the leading of the Holy Spirit.

God doesn't want to hide His will from us. Sometimes we want to know the big picture when God says, "Trust me for the next step."

It worked for Paul. It will work for us.

Holy Spirit, show me the next step I should take in my journey with You. Amen.

Who through the Spirit of holiness was declared with power to be the Son of God by his resurrection from the dead. (Romans 1:4)

This name introduces us to the role the Holy Spirit played in the resurrection of Jesus Christ. The overall idea of Romans 1:4 is clear—By His resurrection from the dead, Jesus was declared (or publicly designated) as the powerful Son of God. It's not that He wasn't the Son of God before the resurrection—He was. But the resurrection serves notice to every skeptic who wonders about Jesus Christ. Is He who He says He is? If He were still dead, we would all wonder about Him. But now Christ has risen from the dead and our questions have been answered.

What role did the Holy Spirit play in the resurrection of Christ? John Owen suggests that the Spirit maintained a watch over the body of Christ while it was in the tomb, preserving it from decay. This would correspond with Psalm 16:10 (quoted by Peter in Acts 2:27 and applied to Jesus). Perhaps the Spirit helped prepare the body of Jesus for the resurrection, providing it with the necessary elements of immortality. This would correspond with the Spirit's role of creation and renewal in the Old Testament.

But the greater point should not be missed. The Son of God has come back from the dead. No one can seriously doubt His claims now. Henceforth those who attack Him must continually stumble at the empty tomb.

At the Garden Tomb in Jerusalem (thought by many people to be the actual location of Jesus' resurrection), one may enter the tomb and see that it is empty. As you make your way out of the area, a sign arrests the eye. Engraved into a wood sign are these words: "He is not here, for He is risen."

Indeed it is true. God the Father promised to raise His Son from the dead. Jesus said in John 10 that He would lay down His own life and then take it up again. Romans 1:4 adds the fact that the Holy Spirit was there on Easter Sunday morning when the greatest moment in human history happened.

Through the Spirit of holiness, God raised Jesus from the dead and declared Him the powerful Son of God.

Very few people have ever died and come back to life. Only one person ever rose from the dead never to die again.

His name is Jesus.

Spirit of God, empower me to declare the Good News that Jesus Christ is alive forevermore. Amen.

No, a man is a Jew if he is one inwardly; and circumcision is circumcision of the heart, by the Spirit, not by the written code. (Romans 2:29)

To some people, circumcision may seem a shocking symbol of the Holy Spirit, but Paul mentioned it several times—in Romans 2:28–29, Philippians 3:3, and Colossians 2:11–12. In Deuteronomy 30:6, Moses predicted that a day would come when Israel would undergo a great national circumcision which would result in changed hearts and a new love for God.

The point of comparison is this—Just as physical circumcision marks a man physically with an outward sign of his relationship to God, even so the Holy Spirit can "circumcise" the heart, giving a person an inward desire to love God and obey His commandments.

Paul never intended to disparage the act of circumcision in Romans 2. After all, God had commanded it in the Old Testament. But like any religious ritual, it tended to lose the spiritual meaning that was always meant to go with it. As a result, many men said, "I must be right with God. After all, I've been circumcised." Many people trust in their baptism in precisely the same way: "I must be a Christian. After all, I've been baptized."

Is baptism wrong? No. But anyone trusting in his baptism to secure his relationship with God is sadly mistaken. Was circumcision wrong? No. But it profited nothing unless the heart was also circumcised.

That's where the Holy Spirit comes in. He alone can give us a new heart and a new love for God. He alone can replace our proud self-righteousness with a humble dependence on God.

In what are you trusting to win approval from God? Church membership? Sunday school attendance? Baptism? Giving to the poor? Good deeds? None of those things matters when it comes to salvation. As good as they are, they are still only outward acts. A person might do those things and still have a hard heart toward God.

What God wants is a heart that is circumcised by the Spirit. When that happens, you will have a new love for God. All that you seek will be given in a moment; all that you have tried to achieve through good works now becomes yours through God's grace.

This is indeed a great miracle, but we should not be surprised. The greatest miracles are those performed by the Holy Spirit within the human heart.

O Lord, tear away anything that keeps me from knowing You. May my heart be made new through the power of Your Spirit. Amen.

SPIRIT OF LIFE IN CHRIST JESUS

Through Christ Jesus the law of the Spirit of life set me free from the law of sin and death.
(Romans 8:2)

This verse states, in extremely simple language, the momentous change wrought in the Christian at the moment of conversion. Every word is crucial but none more so than the little word "free." It describes God's intention in saving you. He wanted to set you free. Whether you knew it or not, before you came to Christ, you were a slave to sin. That's what Paul meant by "the law of sin and death." You sinned because you couldn't help it. And your sin was slowly killing you. The chains of sin were wrapped around your neck, choking off any possibility of knowing God personally.

Through Jesus Christ those chains have been broken—permanently and completely. The things that held you back—your old habits of life, your inner desire to rebel against God, your recurring tendency to engage in self-destructive behavior, your anger and bitterness that seemed to cling like some dirty garments—no longer have the same power over you.

God has set you free from the obligation to obey the urges of the old life. You don't have to live that way any more. In place of the old life with its insatiable urge to do wrong, God has given believers the "Spirit of life in Christ Jesus."

When the Holy Spirit comes in, He brings new life with Him! He replaces the old desires with entirely new ones. In place of the sin that dragged you down, the Holy Spirit begins to lead you to a brand-new way of life. In place of the self-destructive tendencies you once knew, He now gives you a new moral compass.

This change is radical, complete, instantaneous, and frankly, overwhelming for most of us. It's not easy to live one way for thirty years and then suddenly find oneself going in an entirely new direction. It's like a criminal being pardoned after living on death row; he hardly knows what to do with himself.

But the Spirit who gives us life is very patient. Having set us free, He teaches us little by little how to walk with Him, how to follow His leading, and how to experience "life" instead of "death" on a daily basis.

If all this seems mysterious, remember this—You have been set free. The Holy Spirit has liberated you from your old life.

The chains have been broken. You're free!

Free at last! Free at last! Thank God Almighty, I'm free at last! Amen.

SPIRIT OF CHRIST

If anyone does not have the Spirit of Christ, he does not belong to Christ. (Romans 8:9)

This verse gives us a basic distinguishing mark of the Christian. Those who know Christ have the Spirit of Christ within them. Those who don't are completely controlled by the flesh.

Romans 8:5–8 paints a somber portrait of what a life controlled by the flesh looks like:

- Continual desire to do wrong (v. 5)
- Spiritual death (v. 6)
- Hostility to God (v. 7)
- Rebellion against God's law (v. 7)
- Inability to please God (v. 8)

Against those dark tones the new life in the Spirit stands out in bold relief:

- Continual desire to do right (v. 5)
- Daily experience of life and peace (v. 6)

What makes such a dramatic difference? The Holy Spirit living within the believer. He provides the inner transformation that reorients the heart from death to life, from hostility to friendship, and from anger and bitterness to life and peace. The Holy Spirit is God's antidote to the destructive power of the flesh.

All of this is true "if the Spirit of God dwells in you" (v. 9). Some people know the power of the Spirit; others do not. But if we don't know the Spirit, neither do we know the Son, Jesus Christ. That's the implication of Romans 8:9. And everyone who trusts Christ as Savior has the Spirit dwelling within.

The Holy Spirit is called the "Spirit of Christ" because He brings Christ to believers and applies to them the benefits of Christ's atoning death on the cross. At Calvary, Christ won a great victory; the Holy Spirit makes sure that every believer hears the Good News. He takes the things of Christ—His character, His teaching, His resurrection life—and applies them to each individual Christian.

There are many ways to define a Christian. Romans 8:9 offers us this one—A Christian is a person who has the Spirit of Christ dwelling within. If you are worried about whether or not you are a true Christian, ask yourself this question: Have I trusted in Jesus Christ as my Lord and Savior? If the answer is yes, then you may know for certain that the Holy Spirit has taken up residence in your life. You don't have to worry about seeking a feeling. You can simply believe what God has said, and trust the Holy Spirit to lead you to full assurance of your faith.

If you know and love Jesus Christ, you are truly a Christian and the Spirit of Christ now lives in you.

Father, thank You for the Holy Spirit who makes Christ real to me. Amen.

SPIRIT OF HIM WHO RAISED
JESUS FROM THE DEAD

*And if the Spirit of him who raised Jesus from
the dead is living in you, he who raised Christ
from the dead will also give life to your mortal
bodies through his Spirit, who lives in you.*
(Romans 8:11)

In this section of Romans 8, Paul dealt with the reality of the believer's bodily resurrection from the dead. Such a thought is so stupendous, so beyond all human comprehension that we might be forgiven for doubting its truth. How can we know that we will one day be raised from the dead? The answer is this—The same Person who raised Christ from the dead will one day raise us from the dead. Not "the same power" but "the same Person." Our resurrection will be as personal as the resurrection of Jesus Christ. Our faith rests on the promise of God and on His divine performance at the empty tomb on Easter Sunday. If we believe that miracle, then we should have no trouble believing in the miracle that is yet to come—our own bodily resurrection. What God did for Jesus, He will one day do for us.

What connection does the Holy Spirit have with our resurrection? He is the pledge of God that we will one day rise again. Romans 8:11 tells us that if we have the Holy Spirit living in us, we may rest assured that we will one day be raised from the dead. God will "give life" to our dead bodies and He will do it "through His Spirit" who lives in us.

As Charles Hodge points out, this verse cannot mean a merely moral resurrection, as some commentators suggest. In this context, it can only mean that in Christ we have received a complete triumph over death. As He rose physically, so too shall we someday rise from our graves to meet the Lord in the air (1 Thessalonians 4:13–18). It is true that we shall all die eventually, but according to the promise of God, we will not all stay dead. Those who know Jesus will also know the joy of the resurrection from the dead.

Only one question remains. Do you believe this? Perhaps your heart doubts these words. Perhaps you would like to believe but find it exceedingly difficult. Rest your faith on these three pillars: (1) the Father has promised it, (2) the Son has purchased it, and (3) the Spirit has pledged it. All three members of the Trinity unite to guarantee your future.

For believers, death is not the end, but the beginning of all that God has promised us.

Lord Jesus, You showed me the way to victory when You rose from the dead. Grant me strong faith to follow You through death into resurrection and the life everlasting. Amen.

For you did not receive a spirit that makes you a slave again to fear, but you received the Spirit of sonship. (Romans 8:15)

Paul used adoption to picture the way believers become members of the family of God. In Roman law adopted sons lost all rights in their former families and gained full standing in their new families. In particular, adopted sons gained full inheritance rights alongside the natural sons. This truth seemed so wonderful to Paul that he mentioned it several times in the New Testament (Romans 8:23; 9:4; Galatians 4:5). The emphasis each time is on the fact that adopted sons have full rights in the family. They aren't second-class sons, relegated to the back row when family treasures are divided.

In Romans 8:15, Paul contrasted the old "spirit of bondage" with the new "Spirit of sonship." Before coming to Christ, the unbeliever is a slave to sin. Sin rules his life, sin dominates his thoughts, sin controls his motives. Sin is like air; it is his spiritual atmosphere. He lives in fear of the consequences of sin and in fear of the ultimate consequence—death. Sin for the unbeliever is truly a terrible taskmaster.

But all that is changed once a person comes to Jesus Christ. As Romans 6 points out, the believer is now a "slave of righteousness." But this slavery leads to freedom, not to fear and death. In a sense, the believer is now both slave and free. He is a slave to righteousness and free from the chains of sin and death.

The Holy Spirit made this possible through adoption into God's family. When we become Christians, we gain all the rights and privileges that go with that high standing. We can pray; we can go directly into God's presence any time we like; we can search God's Word, be filled with the Spirit, and talk to the Lord directly without going through any human intermediaries.

Most of all, we can now call God "Father." That's the meaning of the Aramaic term *Abba*. It expresses the close, intimate relationship that exists between a father and his children. It's a family term, a word full of love and tenderness.

Think of it. You are no longer a slave, cringing in fear of punishment. You are now a child of God through faith in Jesus Christ. God has adopted you into His family. Do you feel like an outsider? You needn't, for God has granted you full rights as His child, the same as if you had been part of His family forever. You can pray whenever you like and tell God your deepest fears. You can ask Him to give you guidance for the problems you face. You can go to Him any time, night or day, anywhere you like, under any circumstance, without waiting for an invitation. Through Christ you have been given an eternal membership in God's family.

Enjoy it! Use it! Your Father is waiting to hear from you.

How good it is to call You Father. How wonderful to know that You will never turn me away. Amen.

We ourselves, who have the firstfruits of the Spirit, groan inwardly as we wait eagerly for our adoption as sons, the redemption of our bodies. (Romans 8:23)

In the Old Testament, God told the Israelites to bring the "firstfruits" from the harvest—that is, the first-ripened fruits and grains—and present them before the Lord. This offering served two purposes. First, it reminded the people of God that everything they had came directly from God. By giving the first part of the harvest, they were saying, "Lord, we acknowledge that all our blessings come from You." Second, it demonstrated their faith that an even greater harvest was yet to come. They wouldn't give the first if they thought it was the last. They gave the first part because they believed that there was more to come.

The latter meaning was on Paul's mind in Romans 8:23. At the moment a person trusts Christ, the Holy Spirit indwells him. The coming of the Spirit may be likened to the "firstfruits" of the harvest. As wonderful as the Christian life is, it's not the total experience God has for His children. Better things are yet to come. Now, we groan under the struggles of this life. We live in a decaying world, trapped in the bondage of sin. Each week the garbage trucks haul off tons of trash, each week the hospitals add new patients, each week the dentists find new cavities—all of it proof that this is not the world as God created it. Ever since Adam and Eve ate the forbidden fruit, our world has lived under a curse (Genesis 3:17–19). What was easy has become hard. What was meant to last forever now decays and dies.

Including you and me. Our bodies grow old, they lose their shape, our hair changes color, our muscles sag, our eyesight dims, our teeth begin to fall out, our legs won't run as far, our arms lose their strength. It happens to everyone sooner or later. No one is exempt who lives on planet earth. No wonder we groan. Life after Eden is no paradise.

Against all that, God has given us the Holy Spirit as the "firstfruits" of a harvest yet to come. He spells it out in verse 23, "the redemption of our bodies." What does that mean? No one can say for certain, except that we will have a resurrection body like the one Jesus had when He rose from the dead. It's easier to say what we won't have— no more eyeglasses, no more hearing aids, no more wheelchairs, no more false teeth, no more cancer, no more AIDS, no more heart attacks, no more strokes, no more arthritis, no more growing old, no more losing our strength to the passing of years. All of that will be gone forever.

Does it seem like a dream? It's not. Cheer up, child of God. Better days are coming.

Lord Jesus, speed the days until Your return. While I wait, grant me faith to believe that better days are just around the corner. Amen.

In the same way, the Spirit helps us in our weakness. We do not know what we ought to pray for, but the Spirit himself intercedes for us with groans that words cannot express.
(Romans 8:26)

This verse describes a most unique ministry of the Holy Spirit. Romans 8:26 says that "the Spirit helps us in our weakness." The word translated "help" means to come to the aid of someone in desperate need. For example, we are in the stands watching a race when we see a runner faltering in the final turn. He stumbles and is about to fall. Seeing that he is not going to make it, we rush from the stands, come to his side, put our arms around him, and say, "Let us help you to the finish line." That's what the Holy Spirit does for us. He sees when we are in trouble and He comes to our aid.

Have you ever been in a situation so desperate that you couldn't pray? Have you ever been so emotionally exhausted that you tried to pray but the words wouldn't come out? Have you ever been so frightened that all you could do was cry out, "O God?" When we don't know what to say, and all we can do is cry out "O God!" the message is, "Don't worry. That's enough, because the Holy Spirit is praying for you."

We know that Jesus is in heaven praying for us. But Paul goes a step beyond that. When we come to the moment of complete exhaustion and can no longer frame the words, we don't have to worry. The Holy Spirit will pray for us. In our weakness He is strong. When we cannot speak, He speaks for us.

Martin Luther said that it is a good thing if we occasionally receive the opposite of what we pray for, because that's a sign the Holy Spirit is at work in our lives. I find that suggestion to be most encouraging because so many times our prayers—even in our best moments—are tinged with selfish motives. Rarely do we pray from a truly selfless point of view. We may be praying, "Lord, please do this and this and this." Meanwhile the Holy Spirit inside is saying, "Lord, if this person saw the bigger picture, he or she would really ask for such-and-such." As we pray from our weak and limited perspective, the Holy Spirit corrects our prayers so that God's will is always done. Since the Holy Spirit knows God's will, and since He searches our hearts (v. 27), He is able to pray for us in ways that always correspond to God's will. One sign that this is actually happening is when we pray for one thing and God does the opposite.

Does that mean our prayers are in vain? Not at all. Does it mean we shouldn't pray? Not at all. It simply reveals our inherent human weakness and the limitation of our perspective on life. We see the part; the Holy Spirit sees the whole. We see one little piece; the Holy Spirit sees the big picture. We pray according to the little bit that we see; the Holy Spirit prays according to His perfect knowledge.

This truth ought to encourage us to pray boldly, knowing that the Holy Spirit is interceding for us even as we pray for ourselves.

Are we too tired to pray right now? Take heart! The Holy Spirit is praying for us.

Spirit of God, thank You for being there when I truly need You. Amen.

SPIRIT WHO IS FROM GOD

We have not received the spirit of the world but the Spirit who is from God, that we may understand what God has freely given us.
(1 Corinthians 2:12)

Here we have another description of the fundamental difference between Christians and non-Christians. Christians have received "the Spirit who is from God," not "the spirit of the world." Unbelievers may experience various aspects of the Spirit's ministry, principally that of conviction of sin (John 16:8–11). But only believers in Christ truly "receive" the Holy Spirit. We have opened our hearts to Him and He has taken up residence within us. No unbeliever can truthfully say that.

This entire passage (1 Corinthians 2:6–16) expands upon the work of the Holy Spirit in revealing the wisdom of God to us. The rulers of the world have never understood God's wisdom—if they had, they wouldn't have crucified Jesus (vv. 6–8). In fact, the people of the world don't understand what great things "God has prepared for those who love Him" (v. 9). But through the Holy Spirit, who knows the mind of God, we now understand the things of God (vv. 10–13). The unsaved do not understand those things and are in no position to judge spiritual reality (vv. 14–15). But God has given believers the mind of Christ, which enables them to understand the things of God (v. 16).

Have you ever wondered why your unsaved friends and loved ones don't understand you? They can't! It's like explaining the music of Bach to a deaf person or the sculpture of Michelangelo to a blind person. The unsaved lack the capacity to grasp spiritual truth. They may know many facts about the Bible—the details of history or the outline of the life of Christ—but without the Holy Spirit, it is all foolishness to them.

Several important implications can be drawn from this truth. First, don't get angry with those who don't know the Lord. Without the Holy Spirit and the mind of Christ, unbelievers remain in spiritual darkness. Second, ask God to remove their blindness and replace it with the light of the Gospel of Christ. Only the miracle of regeneration can cause a person to understand the things of God. Until then, the person truly cannot "see" God's wisdom. Third, God has given us His Spirit to help us understand His Word. All the wisdom of God is now available to us. If we remain baby Christians, we have only ourselves to blame because the Holy Spirit has been given to enable us to grow to spiritual maturity.

Finally, this passage helps us understand why some of the world's most brilliant people never come to Christ. Brilliance apart from God may win the acclaim of the masses, but God calls the smartest person in the world a fool if he or she refuses to bow the knee before Jesus Christ and proclaim

Him Lord and Savior. Such men and women are to be pitied, not admired. In spite of their great intellects, they have missed the central truth of the universe—"the fear of the Lord is the beginning of knowledge" (Proverbs 1:7). Though they may be very religious and even attend church, without the Holy Spirit, they cannot know God or the things of God.

But there is a positive side to all this. We who believe have received the "Spirit who comes from God." We have been given the key that unlocks the door of heavenly treasures. We may go in any time and learn more about God through His Word. Through the Spirit, we may become wiser than the most learned unbelievers. They may have vast intelligence, but God has given us His Spirit.

Spirit of God, too often I have wasted the precious resources You put within my reach. Open my eyes to see the wonderful things within God's Word. Amen.

But you were washed, you were sanctified, you were justified in the name of the Lord Jesus Christ and by the Spirit of our God.
(1 Corinthians 6:11)

Here we have a wonderful statement about the amazing transformation brought about by Jesus Christ through the work of the Holy Spirit in the human heart. Once again, Paul stressed the tremendous difference between believers and unbelievers. In the future, believers will judge the world (1 Corinthians 6:2), yet in Paul's day, they were taking each other to court in front of unbelievers. This showed how little the Corinthians understood the radical change made by their conversion.

To illustrate this truth, Paul pointed out that many of the Corinthians had come to Christ from deeply sinful lifestyles. Some had been idolaters, some adulterers, some homosexuals, some thieves, some slanderers, some drunkards, and some swindlers. A pretty scurvy lot! But from just such people had God built His church in Corinth. Already Paul had said that not many wise or influential people are chosen for salvation (1 Corinthians 1:26). From this passage, it appears that God went to the other end of the spectrum. He found those who were deeply enmeshed in terrible sins—moral, spiritual, and sexual—and He saved them. He washed them—a reference to cleansing through the blood of Christ. He sanctified them—by declaring them holy in His eyes. He justified them—by declaring them righteous.

He did this "in the name of the Lord Jesus"—that is, on the basis of His divine merit, and "by the Spirit of our God." Their lives were utterly transformed by Jesus Christ through the regenerating ministry of the Holy Spirit.

This truth deserves some consideration. It is popular in our day to dismiss sinful behavior as "in-born" or "constitutional" or "genetic"; thus, not morally wrong or at least impossible to change. "God made me this way," sinners cry aloud. No, God didn't make us that way. We made ourselves the way we are by following the dictates of our sinful natures.

Can drunkards change? Thank God, the answer is yes. What about homosexuals? Yes, they too can change. Must thieves live forever tormented by an incurable desire to steal? No, they don't have to stay that way. The same is true of every other kind of sinner.

We can change, or more precisely, God can change us through a life-changing encounter with Jesus Christ by the power of the Holy Spirit. No one needs to live in sin forever. No one who has the slightest desire for a new life is ever beyond the grace of God.

Let the saints of God rejoice in this—What we were, we are no more. Through Jesus Christ, deep radical reorientation is possible.

The Holy Spirit has come not only to make the change, but to enable us to have brand-new lives.

Father, forgive me for doubting Your power to change lives today. Thank You for not giving up on me when I was still living in sin. Amen.

Do you not know that your body is a temple of the Holy Spirit, who is in you, whom you have received from God? (1 Corinthians 6:19)

Why do some Christians think that it doesn't matter how we live as long as we are saved? Why do some people claim to accept Christ in childhood and then go for years without following Him? How can a true Christian ever commit sexual immorality? These issues are all addressed in 1 Corinthians 6:19–20. Paul used the image of the Old Testament temple to help us understand the indwelling of the Holy Spirit. During those days, the temple represented the presence of God with His people. When the Israelites passed by the Temple Mount, they thought, God is in this place. Even the pagans of other nations understood that the God of Israel dwelt with His people in the temple at Jerusalem. The temple stood as a visible reminder that God was not far off in the heavens, but had chosen to live among His people.

Today there is no one building that Christians look to as the temple. Even though church buildings are sometimes called "the house of God," they aren't temples in the Old Testament sense. Since God doesn't dwell in buildings nowadays, where can we find Him?

The answer to that question is that God now dwells in His people. This is a vast change from Old Testament days. When Solomon was king, ev-

147

eryone journeyed to Jerusalem to worship at the temple. But all that has changed. Every Christian man is a temple of God. Every Christian woman is a temple of God. All true Christians are the temples of God today.

So how many temples does God have today? Multiplied millions, because every child of God is a temple of God. Think of what that means. We are temples of God! Almighty God has come to live in us. We carry with us, wherever we go, the name of God, the testimony of God, the Spirit of God, and the presence of God.

How then can any believer continue living in sin? How can a Christian commit adultery? It is simply unthinkable for those who understand the high calling of being God's temple. To continue in sin after coming to Christ is like pouring raw sewage down the aisles of a Gothic cathedral.

These are strong words, but Paul used this image in his warning against sexual immorality. Remember, God's Spirit goes with you wherever you go. He is there when you rise, when you dress, when you eat, when you drink, when you speak on the phone, when you watch TV, when you drive your car. Everywhere you go, God's Spirit goes with you. You cannot escape Him for He lives within you.

Therefore, honor God with your body. Don't drag the Lord's reputation into the mud by what you see, what you say, where you go, or what you do.

You are God's temple. It's a high calling and an awesome responsibility that must not be taken lightly.

Holy Spirit, You have made us Your dwelling place. Make us mindful of Your presence in everything we do. Amen.

There are different kinds of gifts, but the same Spirit. (1 Corinthians 12:4)

The New Testament speaks of spiritual gifts given to every believer. These are supernatural abilities (often but not always combined with natural talents) that enable the believer to function effectively in the body of Christ. A list of some of the gifts is found in 1 Corinthians 12:7–11: wisdom, knowledge, faith, healing, miraculous powers, prophecy, the ability to distinguish spirits, speaking in tongues, and the interpretation of tongues. Later in this same chapter, Paul mentioned apostleship, prophecy, teaching, helps, and administration. He offered two other lists in Romans 12 and Ephesians 4. In 1 Peter 4:10–11, we find all spiritual gifts divided into two general categories: speaking and serving. Since no one list is complete, it is likely that other spiritual gifts may be given as the Holy Spirit deems appropriate.

In 1 Corinthians 12–14, Paul was largely concerned with the use and abuse of spiritual gifts—especially the gift of tongues. He emphasized in Chapter 12 that although there are many gifts, they all come from the same Spirit. Each one has its own purpose in the body of Christ. Perhaps some had special significance in the early years of the Christian church. Some may be found in one church but not in another, according to the sovereign will of the Holy Spirit. No one person will have all the gifts, and all the gifts given to an individual will not necessarily be evident at the same time.

These points—which seem quite elementary—must continually be restated because of our human tendency to compare ourselves to each other. Those with the gift of faith may have little patience with the careful administrators. Teachers may frustrate helpers, and prophets may upset servants. Because we are all by nature rather self-centered, it is easy to use ourselves as the standard for measuring other believers.

Gift-comparison is foolish because it downplays the value of the contributions made by others and denies the sovereignty of God. The Holy Spirit distributes spiritual gifts to the body of Christ as He determines.

We may draw several conclusions from this. First, no gift is superior to any other gift since all gifts come from the same Spirit. Second, while gifts differ in function and form, their purpose is always the same—to build up the body of Christ. Third, your "gift mix" is God's perfect design for you, taking into consideration your background, natural abilities, and place of maximum contribution to the church. Each believer has a spiritual gift, and doubtless many believers have several gifts in varying proportions. Fourth, envy has no place in the body of Christ since the gifts come solely from the Lord. Finally, unity is paramount since all gifts come from the same Spirit.

Finally, spiritual gifts are given to be used—not abused or neglected. If you wish to find the place where you "fit" in God's kingdom, you need to make it a priority to discover your spiritual gifts. Too many believers struggle because they serve in areas and ministries for which they are not gifted.

Here are three signs that you have discovered your "gift mix." As you use the gifts, you will experience great personal satisfaction, a measure of spiritual success, and recognition from other believers that you are indeed doing what God called you to do.

Have you taken the time to discover your spiritual gifts?

Spirit of God, show me how I can use my unique gifts to serve others for Jesus' sake. Amen.

ONE SPIRIT

For we were all baptized by one Spirit into one body—whether Jews or Greeks, slave or free—and we were all given the one Spirit to drink.
(1 Corinthians 12:13)

There is one Holy Spirit. He is the one who baptizes us into the body of Christ. Everyone comes to Christ the same way—by faith. Everyone is forgiven the same way—by the blood of the cross. Everyone comes into the body of Christ the same way—by the Holy Spirit.

God doesn't have two ways of salvation, two methods of forgiveness, two bodies of Christ, or two Holy Spirits—one for the "minor" gifts and one for the "major" gifts. All true Christians share the same Holy Spirit. There is no secondary position in the body of Christ.

This concept needs to be emphasized in a day when the body of Christ has fragmented into so many groups—some built around a particular doctrine or beloved leader, others around some spectacular spiritual gift, still others around a national heritage or ethnic origin. Differences aren't wrong or bad, nor is it necessary for all Christians to believe precisely the same things on issues of lesser importance. We certainly don't have to attend the same church or join the same denomination. God made us different and gave us different gifts as demonstrated in 1 Corinthians 12–14. We ought to celebrate our uniqueness, not apologize for it.

However, we can go so far in stressing our uniqueness that we begin to believe that our group is just a little better than some other Christian group. Surely we don't mean to slide into a kind of twentieth-century gnosticism where we think we have received some "special revelation" not given to other Christians. But it can happen. When it does, we have moved away from the faith of the New Testament.

The body of Christ has many parts—eyes, ears, feet, hands, and the many internal organs necessary for survival. If the eye says, "I don't need the hand" or if the elbow says, "Forget about the ear," the whole body suffers. We need each other, and everyone else in the body needs us!

Since we all came into the body of Christ through the "one Spirit," we ought to remain united in love despite our many differences. And we ought to hold our convictions in love, treating other believers with respect.

In the body of Christ, it's OK to be different, but it's not OK to think that being different makes you better than someone else.

Spirit of God, teach me to love other Christians, especially the ones who seem most unlike me. Amen.

*You show that you are a letter from Christ, the
result of our ministry, written not with ink but
with the Spirit of the living God, not on tablets
of stone, but on tablets of human hearts.*
(2 Corinthians 3:3)

The apostle Paul was not without his critics, whether from Jewish opponents outside the church or
from certain people inside the church. In this case,
he was evidently being criticized in Corinth for being a relentless self-promoter (a charge far from
the truth) who did not offer any letters of commendation from the Jerusalem church to back up
his claim to apostolic authority.

Paul was not opposed to using such letters. In
fact, he followed the practice when the need arose.
But false teachers had befuddled the Corinthians
by offering their own letters of commendation and
then attacking Paul for not having such letters.
Thus the church had become confused concerning Paul's ministry. Was he really an apostle of the
Lord? Could he be trusted? Why didn't he offer letters of commendation?

Paul's answer was simple and most revealing.
The Corinthians themselves were his "letter of rec-
ommendation." During his ministry in Corinth, the
power of the Gospel had radically changed many
lives. Thieves stopped stealing, drunkards stopped
drinking, adulterers became faithful spouses, and
homosexuals gave up their sinful practices. As the
Gospel triumphed in one heart after another, the

new Christians became the best possible proof of the legitimacy of Paul's ministry.

The false teachers could preach all they wanted and offer all the forged letters they could find, but their message had no life-transforming power. Paul's did, because it offered the Gospel of Christ and the ministry of the Holy Spirit to change lives from the inside out.

In essence, Paul said to the Corinthians, "You are my letter, written by Jesus Christ." The writing was not with ink (which would eventually fade), but with the Spirit of the living God (which would last forever). It was not on tablets of stone (which might be lost or broken), but on tablets of human hearts (which could never be misplaced or stolen). This powerful imagery rests on the promise of the new covenant, in which God promised to write His law within the human heart (Jeremiah 31:31–34).

Think about the familiar question: "If you were arrested for being a Christian, would there be enough evidence to convict you?" The ultimate defense of your faith rests not in your church membership or in your baptism, but in the daily demonstration of a changed life through the power of the Holy Spirit. If your life is no different from the people around you, how will anyone know that you are truly born again?

The measure of your effectiveness is the lives that Christ is changing through your personal witness. How is your street different, your school different, your workplace different, because you are there?

The world doesn't understand theology, but everyone understands the testimony of a truly changed life. That happens not through religion, but through the power of the Holy Spirit.

When the change is obvious, we won't need anyone to back up our words. We will be living proof that Jesus Christ is alive today.

Spirit of the living God, make the change so obvious that no one can doubt that Jesus truly lives in me. Amen.

And we, who with unveiled faces all reflect the Lord's glory, are being transformed into his likeness with ever-increasing glory, which comes from the Lord, who is the Spirit.
(2 Corinthians 3:18)

In 2 Corinthians 3, the temporary character of the old covenant is contrasted with the permanent and far more glorious character of the new covenant. Whereas the glory on Moses' face slowly faded away, the glory of the new covenant is both greater and everlasting. In the end, the Mosaic covenant could only bring death because no man could ever keep the demands of the law perfectly. Anyone trying to find salvation through the law was thus doomed to failure, frustration, and (ultimately) death. The law brings death (v. 6) in the sense that while it pointed the way to life, no one could keep it perfectly, so the end result was always death.

On the other hand, salvation through Jesus Christ brings life through the Spirit. This is "life" because the Holy Spirit writes the law of God within the human heart. The law failed because no one could keep it. God solved that problem by sending the Holy Spirit to indwell every believer, thus imparting a new desire to please God in all things.

External solutions would not work. The human race didn't need more commandments and prohibitions. No one could obey the ones that had already been given. Only an internal transformation of the heart could change the human situation from death to life. This God accomplished through the new covenant, which was made possible by the death of Christ, whose benefits are brought to the believer by the indwelling Holy Spirit.

When Paul said, "The Lord, who is the Spirit," was he confusing the persons of the Trinity? No. Instead, he was affirming the full deity of the Holy Spirit. Similar terms are often used for the Son and the Spirit because they are one in purpose. Christ comes to the believer through the ministry of the Holy Spirit. Said another way, the Holy Spirit acts as the "agent" of the Son, accomplishing His divine purposes.

God intends that through the ministry of the Spirit we might be made into the image of Jesus Christ. But we have a blessing the Old Testament believers never had—we see Jesus Christ with unveiled faces. Nothing stands between the Christian and the Lord. Through the Holy Spirit we are daily being transformed into "His likeness" with ever-increasing glory. This process of sanctification goes on every single day as the Spirit uses the experiences of life to make us more like Jesus.

The process is never finished in this life; no one can ever say, "I'm just like Jesus." But the Spirit never ceases to lead us slowly toward the goal of making us more like Christ.

Spirit of God, make me more like Jesus today. Amen.

*He redeemed us in order that the blessing
given to Abraham might come to the Gentiles
through Christ Jesus, so that by faith we might
receive the promise of the Spirit.*
(Galatians 3:14)

About four thousand years ago, God promised to
bless Abraham and through him to bless the entire
world (Genesis 12:1–3). From that single promise
came the nation of Israel and the Messiah, Jesus
Christ. Across the generations, God successively
clarified the promise by spelling out its various
provisions, including a specific land for Israel, a
king for Israel, and a new covenant for Israel.

Included in the new covenant were provisions
for an inner change of heart. But Paul's point in
Galatians 3:14 is that God always intended to ex-
tend these blessings to the Gentiles as well as to
the Jews. This thought shocked many Jews of the
first century, who saw themselves as the exclusive
recipients of God's grace. To suggest that the Gentiles might stand on an equal basis with the Jews
was unthinkable. It offended their sense of racial
and moral superiority.

But the Gentiles were part of God's plan from
the beginning. That's why Genesis 12:3 specifies
that through Abraham "all peoples" would be
blessed. God never wanted to save only one nation or one race or one ethnic group. His heart en-
compassed all the nations of the world. In the Old
Testament, Israel was meant to be a light to the

Gentiles. Even then, proselytes from the surrounding nations could join themselves to the nation of Israel and become worshipers of the one true God.

In Jesus Christ, all national boundaries are broken down. Anyone, anywhere and at any time, can become a Christian. When they do, they receive the "blessing" promised to Abraham—the blessing of eternal salvation. Not only that, but they also receive "the promise" of the Holy Spirit. He enters their hearts, bringing new life and a new desire to serve God.

So today no one needs to become a Jew in order to be saved. But no one needs to become an American either. You can be saved right where you are, without leaving your country or learning another language or undergoing religious rituals of any kind. God has made salvation simple so that it might be freely available to the entire world.

Who are the true children of Abraham? Those who believe in Jesus, the ultimate son of Abraham. Abraham was justified by faith, the same as believers today. It is not works that commend us to God, but simple, childlike faith in God's Son.

Though thousands of years separate us from Abraham, he is still the father of all those who are saved by faith.

Heavenly Father, thank You for including the whole world in Your great plan of salvation. Help me to take seriously Your call to take the Gospel to those who have never heard it. Amen.

SPIRIT OF HIS SON
===

*Because you are sons, God sent the Spirit of his
Son into our hearts, the Spirit who calls out,
"Abba, Father."* (Galatians 4:6)

Would a freed slave ever go back to bondage? To
us, the answer seems obvious, but it wasn't so
clear to the first-century Christians in Galatia. Many
of them were in danger of stepping back into the
bondage of legalism after having been set free by
Jesus Christ.

How could such a thing happen? Evidently certain false teachers had spread a message that mixed
the law of the Old Testament with the Gospel of
Jesus Christ. That deadly mixture perverted the
doctrine of grace and denied the truth of justification by faith. As Christians drank that deadly poi-
son, they found their faith being destroyed.

Legalism always does that. By substituting human works for the pure grace of God, it puts believers on an impossible performance standard.
Although intended to bring people closer to God,
it actually pushes them farther away because the
legalist stresses outward behavior instead of inner
dependence on the Holy Spirit.

In Galatians 4, Paul illustrated the truth about
justification with a comparison between slaves and
heirs. When a child is young, he or she is no different from a slave—even though the child is an
heir to the father's estate (v. 1). A child has no
freedom and can make no decisions on his or her

own. A child lives under the tutelage of guardians and trustees. This continues until the time set by a father when the child will finally come of age (v. 2).

Unbelievers are like slaves, in bondage to all forms of religious teaching, none of which lead to salvation. Some people do good works, others light candles, still others join cults. But none of it matters when it comes to salvation (v. 3). Without Christ, all of us live in bondage.

God solved that problem by sending His Son to the world at just the right time (v. 4). Two great results flow to us as a result of Christ's coming to the world (v. 5). First, we are completely set free from the old system of rules and commandments. Second, we now receive the "full rights" of sons and daughters. All the benefits of salvation are now given to those who believe in Jesus Christ.

Because we are His children and not slaves, God sent the "Spirit of His Son" into our hearts. No longer does God seem like a harsh taskmaster, asking of us what we can never produce. Now we call God "Father" or "Daddy" (which is what the term *Abba* implies). The legalist doesn't call God "Father" because the relationship is built on law, not on love. Only when we know our relationship with God is secure can we truly call Him "Father."

That's the wonderful miracle of grace. Through the Holy Spirit's work in our hearts, we now call God "Father." He's there whenever we need Him; we don't have to make an appointment or worry whether He will be glad to speak to us.

He's our Father. Why not stop and talk to Him right now?

Father, thank You for using such a sweet, simple word to describe who You are. With You as my Father, I have nothing to fear. Amen.

SEAL

*Having believed, you were marked in him with
a seal, the promised Holy Spirit.*
(Ephesians 1:13)

The word "seal" refers to an official mark placed
on a document (such as the mark of a signet ring
on soft wax) indicating both the owner of the document and guaranteeing its security. In the ancient
world, seals served as legal tokens of ownership
and authority. To place a seal on a document
meant that the power of the one making the seal
stood behind the seal itself.

As an illustration we may think of a certified letter, which is sealed by the sender and may be
opened only by the designated recipient. Any un-
authorized opening would be subject to the pen-
alty of law. For a related biblical illustration, we
might remember that Pilate ordered the tomb of
Christ sealed in order to deter possible grave rob-
bers. In that case, the seal may not have been
more than a string with a wax mark indicating that
the power of imperial Rome stood behind the order to seal the tomb.

In Ephesians 1:13, the Holy Spirit is the seal of
our salvation. He is the "proof" that we belong to
Jesus Christ. God has "marked" us with the Holy
Spirit, who now lives within is. Ephesians 4:30
adds the thought that we are "sealed for the day of
redemption"—a reference to the second coming
of Jesus Christ. This thought ought to encourage

our hearts. Many believers struggle with the assurance of salvation, wondering if they have been "good enough" to finally be saved. The answer, of course, is that no one can ever be "good enough" in God's sight. That's why Christ came to the world in the first place. He came for those who were not "good enough," so that through His perfect goodness, we might be saved.

Therefore, we may say frankly that God wants us to have the full assurance of our salvation without regard to our personal feelings. If we are truly born again, God has sealed us with the Holy Spirit as a present reminder that we belong to Christ and as a guarantee of our future deliverance when Jesus returns.

If this seems confusing, think again of the illustration of a certified letter. No one can open it except the sender or the receiver. But since God is the sender, sealer, and receiver, our salvation must be eternally secure. If you are saved, the devil himself can't break the seal of the Holy Spirit. No power except God's power can make or break the seal. Therefore, we can rest assured that if we have trusted Christ, we will one day end up in heaven.

Dr. Hoehner summarizes the matter this way— God is the one who seals us, Christ is the sphere in which the sealing is done, and the Holy Spirit is the instrument of the seal. All three persons of the Trinity are involved in the process. We can't be more secure than that.

Gracious Father, forgive me for doubting Your good intentions. Sometimes I look too much to myself and not enough to Your clear promises. Help me to rest in the certainty of my salvation. Amen.

DEPOSIT

*Who is a deposit guaranteeing our inheritance
until the redemption of those who are God's
possession—to the praise of his glory.*
(Ephesians 1:14)

Anyone who has ever purchased a house or a car
understands the concept of a deposit. When a
person signs a contract, he puts down "earnest
money" so that the seller knows he is serious.
Once the contract has been accepted, if the buyer
changes his mind, he loses the "earnest money."

The deposit not only shows a buyer's serious-
ness, it also guarantees that he fully intends to pay
the rest of the money. That is, a deposit is more
than a "pledge" of good intentions. A deposit is a
legally binding commitment which an individual
may forfeit under certain conditions.

Therefore, money managers often tell people to
be very careful about making deposits. If you don't
want the car, you shouldn't put any money down.
If you don't want the house, you need to keep your
checkbook in your pocket. A deposit is serious
business.

That's why this symbol is so important. The
Holy Spirit is God's "deposit" in our lives, guaranteeing He will one day finish what He has started.
By giving us the Spirit, God has made a down payment on our future salvation.

Think about the great blessings that are already
ours because we have the Holy Spirit: indwelling,

intercession, comfort, guidance, security, full rights as the children of God, the Spirit of Christ within us, the fruit of the Spirit, the power of the Spirit, the hope of the Spirit, to name only a few. Yet these things—as good as they are—are only the down payment (or "firstfruits") of what God will yet do for us.

For those who know the Lord, it only gets better from here on out. We have many blessings from God, and what we have received is only a paltry pittance of what God intends to shower upon us.

Will God take care of His children? Yes, He will. Will He keep His promises? Yes, He will. Will He one day make us fully into the image of Christ? Yes, He will. These words are not idle speculation. He gave us the Holy Spirit to guarantee the complete fulfillment of every part of every promise.

The Holy Spirit is the "first installment" of our salvation. His presence in our lives guarantees that the blessings we receive today are but a foretaste of what God will one day reveal to us. Though we may often doubt it, God always finishes what He starts. He will complete the work of redemption.

Hold onto that thought, Christian. God finishes what He starts. We can count on that.

Almighty God, in a world filled with broken promises, it's good to know that You are a God who finishes what You start. I am counting on You. Amen.

SPIRIT OF
WISDOM AND REVELATION

I keep asking that the God of our Lord Jesus Christ, the glorious Father, may give you the Spirit of wisdom and revelation.
(Ephesians 1:17)

One of the most important ministries of the Holy Spirit is to teach us the things of God. He not only teaches us who God is, but how He works and what His character is like. Paul's prayer in Ephesians 1:15–23 gives us valuable insight into how the Spirit does His work.

Although every believer has the Holy Spirit as a permanent possession, not every believer experiences the full effect of His ministry. Paul prayed that his readers would experience the Holy Spirit's fullness in their relationship to God. Wisdom refers to a general understanding of who God is, while revelation focuses on the special insight the Spirit gives into the divine mysteries of God. A comparable passage might be Psalm 103:7, "He made known His ways to Moses, His deeds to the people of Israel." Moses had a deeper knowledge of God than the average Israelite. While the entire nation experienced God's miraculous power at the Red Sea, only Moses ascended Mt. Sinai to speak with God face to face.

So it is in the Christian life. To every Christian is given the privilege of knowing God personally. But only those who seek true intimacy with God ever find it. Just as there are different levels of knowing ("I know who George Washington is" vs. "I know my wife"), even so there are different levels of the knowledge of God.

Paul's prayer asked God to grant the Ephesians both a general knowledge of who He is and a deeper understanding of His great purposes in history. The apostle desired that all Christians should attain this deeper understanding through the Holy Spirit.

Ephesians 1:17 also gives us the purpose of experiencing the fullness of the Holy Spirit: "That you may know [God] better." This is always the result of the Holy Spirit's work. He comes to introduce us to God—His person, His righteous character, His saving acts in history, and His divine plan for mankind. The Greek word for "know" speaks less of intellectual knowledge and more of a deep, personal, practical knowledge of God. In contrast to those worldly philosophies that say, "Know yourself," Christianity says, "Know God first and foremost, for in knowing God, you will truly know yourself."

Here, then, are some useful questions to measure our spiritual growth: Do we know God better today than we did this time last year? What have we learned about God's character in the last twelve months? How much have we grown in our understanding of God's plan for the world?

Too often we measure our Christianity in purely personal terms: "I'm handling my problems a lot better now," "I don't get angry as quickly as I used to," "We almost got a divorce, but we didn't." As good as those things are, they pale against the deeper knowledge of God, for in knowing God rightly, all those other advancements will eventually take place.

The chief thing is to know God. The great ministry of the Holy Spirit is to help us know God better. Let us therefore press on to know the Lord, for in knowing Him, we will discover the answers to all our other questions—or we will discover that the questions weren't that important in the first place.

Spirit of wisdom and revelation, show me that first things must come first. Teach me more about God. Amen.

HOLY SPIRIT OF GOD

And do not grieve the Holy Spirit of God, with whom you were sealed for the day of redemption. (Ephesians 4:30)

This verse tells us that the Holy Spirit is a divine person, not merely an influence or impersonal power. Only a person can be grieved. An influence has no feelings; a power has no emotions. Since the Holy Spirit is the third member of the Trinity, He possesses the qualities of true personhood, including the ability to feel anger, joy, sorrow, and grief.

The Holy Spirit grieves when God's children harbor anger and bitterness. Ephesians 4:29 mentions "unwholesome talk" as one thing that grieves the Spirit. In verse 31, we find six additional negative outward expressions: bitterness, rage, anger, brawling, slander, and malice. Unwholesome talk is a general category that includes unwarranted criticism, lying, dirty jokes, angry retorts, and salacious gossip. Bitterness is the expression of hostility toward those who have hurt us. Rage refers to a deep, settled hatred for someone. Anger is the heated emotion of disgust at what another person has said or done. Brawling results as anger builds up to physical violence. Slander covers such things as character assassination, lying under oath, telling the truth in such a way as to hurt another person, and spreading lies. Malice refers to a general harboring of dislike toward other people.

We may sum up these words by saying that the Holy Spirit of God is very sensitive to the way we treat other people. He listens to our words, monitors our thoughts, and tracks our emotions. The Spirit also judges our motives. He knows when we mean to hurt someone else by our actions. He is not deceived by the little games we play to cover our unkindness.

Nothing is hidden from Him. When we mistreat others, the Spirit is grieved and His power in our life is diminished. What are the marks that we have grieved the Holy Spirit? We experience a sense of loss, an inner sense that things aren't right between the Lord and ourselves. A gnawing conviction of sin makes us uncomfortable until we deal with it.

Unless we treat others with Christian love, we cannot expect to know the full blessing of God. Unkind words, malicious thoughts, a bitter spirit —these things clog the channel of God's blessing. Until we deal with the problem, the channel will remained clogged and closed.–

It won't do any good to pray and beg God for the help of the Holy Spirit. Going to church or doing good works won't make things better. It is only as we confess our sins that our relationship with God is restored.

We may treat this in a rather academic fashion or we may take seriously the truth that the Holy Spirit of God is a person whom we may please or grieve, depending solely on the way we treat others.

Perhaps it would be good to do a "relationship inventory" based on Ephesians 4:29–32. Are we grieving or pleasing the Holy Spirit by the way we treat others?

Gracious Father, make me sensitive to the inner promptings of Your Spirit. Help me to know when You are grieved by my behavior so that I may quickly make things right. Amen.

WINE

Do not get drunk on wine, which leads to
debauchery. Instead, be filled with the Spirit.
(Ephesians 5:18)

Wine is one of the most unusual symbols of the
Holy Spirit. In two New Testament passages, a
contrast is drawn between the effects of wine and
the effects of the Holy Spirit. On the Day of Pentecost the Holy Spirit came in great force on the assembly of believers (Acts 2). Supernatural signs
accompanied the descent of the Spirit—a sound
like a rushing wind, the appearance of something
like tongues of fire, and the miraculous ability to
speak in other tongues for the proclamation of
biblical truth. This last manifestation captured the
attention of the multitudes of Jews who had gathered in Jerusalem for Pentecost. They were stunned
to hear relatively uneducated men from Galilee
speak fluently in foreign tongues they had never
known before. Evidently the disciples spoke in at
least fifteen languages or dialects that day. Un-
deniably, something unusual had happened.

But as is often the case when unbelievers encounter the work of God, they tried to explain it in
purely natural terms. They thought the disciples
had been drinking too much and were babbling
under the influence of alcohol. The first words of
Peter's sermon disputed this reasoning: "These
men are not drunk, as you suppose. It's only nine
in the morning!" (Acts 2:15) He went on to say that

what had happened was a fulfillment (partially, at least) of Joel 2:28–32, which predicted a universal outpouring of God's Spirit in the "last days."

Note that unbelievers confused the coming of the Spirit with the power of wine. A similar comparison occurs in Ephesians 5:18: "Do not get drunk on wine, which leads to debauchery. Instead, be filled with the Spirit." What precisely is the point of contrast between wine and the Holy Spirit? Doubtless the issue is influence or control. A person under the influence of wine experiences altered behavior. He may say or do things he would not ordinarily do. Emotions may be heightened for a brief period, causing the person to experience anger followed quickly by elation followed quickly by depression. If the person drinks enough wine, his or her mental processes will be affected and decision-making ability radically altered—almost always with a negative result.

Likewise, the filling of the Holy Spirit produces a change in behavior. In Acts, once-timid disciples became flaming evangelists. In Ephesians 5:19–21, Paul mentioned three practical results of the filling of the Spirit: singing, a thankful heart, and an attitude of mutual submission. The last result is most significant, because true submission always involves giving up one's right to be in control in every situation. When we submit from the heart, we are saying, "I don't have to have my way all the time." Only a heart touched by the Holy Spirit can maintain such an attitude.

Two other biblical passages also shed light on this symbol. When Jesus warned against putting new wine in old wineskins (Matthew 9:16–17), He was teaching us that the new Gospel of grace could never be contained within the old forms of the law. In John 2, Jesus turned water into wine at the wedding feast in Cana. This miracle not only demonstrated Jesus' power over nature, it also confirmed the joy that Jesus brings to human life through the transforming ministry of the Holy Spirit. Whereas Moses turned water into blood as a sign of God's judgment (Exodus 7:14–24), Jesus turned water into wine as a sign that salvation has come at last to the world.

Thus, there is both a positive and negative meaning to wine as it relates to the Holy Spirit. Negatively, wine may control the human mind and body, leading to drunkenness and debauchery. Positively, it pictures the joy that Jesus Christ brings when His salvation comes to the human heart. It also points to the change that is possible when the Holy Spirit fills us.

When the police arrest someone for driving while intoxicated, the charge is in some states called DUI—Driving Under the Influence. Perhaps we should pray to be found LUI—Living Under the Influence of the Holy Spirit.

Spirit of God, I have lived too long under my own control. Fill me now so that I may live under Your divine influence. Amen.

For I know that through your prayers and the help given by the Spirit of Jesus Christ, what has happened to me will turn out for my deliverance. (Philippians 1:19)

Philippians is called a "prison epistle" because Paul wrote it while incarcerated in Rome. Upon his arrival there, he was put under house arrest, pending his trial before Caesar. Although he was in chains and under heavy guard, he was free to receive visitors and to share Christ as he pleased. Evidently, some of his guards had trusted Christ as a result of his witness (Philippians 4:22) and many Christians had taken courage by his example of grace under pressure.

However, not everything was well. He was, after all, in prison. He could not foresee the eventual result of his trial, which might result in his release, further imprisonment, or possible death (Philippians 1:20–24). Though he felt excited at the prospect of seeing Jesus face to face, Paul knew that he could help many more people if he stayed alive. Furthermore, some people were taking advantage of his imprisonment to preach Christ from wrong motives, hoping to stir up trouble for Paul in prison.

In spite of these frustrations, Paul rejoiced. How does a man in jail manifest the joy of the Lord? How did he rise above the humiliation, the confinement, and the difficult living conditions to keep on smiling? Philippians 1:19 points out two answers to those questions. First, Paul rejoiced because of the prayers offered up on his behalf. The very fact that others were praying for him lifted his spirits. Second, he rejoiced because of the help given by "the Spirit of Jesus Christ." This particular title may mean that during Paul's imprisonment, the Holy Spirit made Christ very real to him. Later in Philippians 3:10, Paul spoke of his great desire to know Christ in a deeper and more profound way. He wanted to know the "power of His resurrection" and "the fellowship of sharing in His sufferings." That meant entering deeply into the suffering that comes to all those who follow Jesus and experiencing the power of resurrection life that Christ gives to His followers.

Certainly during his long months in Rome, Paul learned much about what it means to suffer as a Christian. He also discovered in a new way how Christ could give him the power to overcome even in those painful circumstances. As the Holy Spirit worked in his life, Paul learned that, even though he was in chains, he could do "everything" through the power of Christ within (Philippians 4:13).

Here is yet another ministry of the Holy Spirit to believers. He makes Christ real to us in times of suffering and hardship. Sometimes our greatest spiritual growth comes in the darkest moments of life. That should not surprise us since our Lord was a "man of sorrows and acquainted with grief"

(Isaiah 53:3 KJV). Jesus knows all about tears, because He shed so many during His days on the earth. He knows about suffering, because He experienced it firsthand when He hung on the cross.

Following Jesus may lead us to some very agonizing circumstances. But through those terrible experiences, the Holy Spirit can lead us closer to and teach us more about Jesus Christ.

Nothing is wasted for the child of God. All things have meaning, and the difficulties and disappointments in our lives may lead us to deeper experiences of Christ.

Living Lord, how many times have I doubted Your good purposes. Thank You for using my doubts to teach me more about Yourself. Amen.

*He appeared in a body, was vindicated by the
Spirit, was seen by angels, was preached
among the nations, was believed on in the
world, was taken up in glory.* (1 Timothy 3:16)

This verse refers to the work of the Holy Spirit in
authenticating Christ through His miracles and ultimately His resurrection from the dead. When the
Pharisees accused Christ of performing miracles
by the power of the devil, He replied that blasphemy
against the Son could be forgiven, but not blasphemy against the Holy Spirit (Matthew 12:32).
Such an accusation could only come from a heart
utterly closed to all spiritual truth. Because the
miracles of Christ could only have come from the
Holy Spirit, they authenticated His claim to be the
Son of God and the Messiah of Israel.

When Peter preached on the day of Pentecost
(Acts 2:14–40), he explained how Christ was vindicated by His resurrection. Wicked men put Christ
to death by nailing Him to the cross (Acts 2:23).
However, God raised Him from the dead, fulfilling
the promise of Psalm 16:8–11 (Acts 2:24–28). King
David died and is still dead, but Jesus is alive, a
fact witnessed by many people (Acts 2:29–32). He
is now exalted to God's right hand and has sent
the "promised Holy Spirit" to the people of God
(Acts 2:33–34). Peter draws his inescapable conclusion in Acts 2:36: "God has made this Jesus,
whom you crucified, both Lord and Christ" (italics

added). This italicized phrase is most important because Peter was preaching to the very men who had joined with the great mob that put Jesus to death. These men had seen Him as a great threat, an enemy of Israel, an evil man to be destroyed. But God raised up Jesus—a fact they could not deny.

Thus, Christ was vindicated by His resurrection. His bodily resurrection proves that He truly is the Son of God from heaven. Not only that, it establishes His right to be both Lord and Savior.

A dead Christ can save no one. If Jesus is still in the grave, then we are truly the most miserable people in the world, for we have believed a lie. Instead of being saved, we are simply deceived.

That's why the apostles appealed again and again to the resurrection of Jesus. Christianity stands or falls on the singular truth that Jesus Christ rose from the dead. As the hymnwriter put it, "Up from the grave He arose, with a mighty triumph o'er His foes." Indeed He did. Therefore, our faith is secure because it rests on the firm foundation of the bodily resurrection of Christ.

We may believe His words—all of them—because through the Holy Spirit, Jesus has been completely vindicated.

Father, thank You for giving me a faith that is based on fact. Fill my heart with Easter joy, because I know that my Redeemer lives today. Amen.

SPIRIT OF POWER,
LOVE, AND SELF-DISCIPLINE

For God did not give us a spirit of timidity, but a spirit of power, of love, and of self-discipline.
(2 Timothy 1:7)

Paul's final recorded letter in the New Testament is 2 Timothy. The year was approximately A.D. 66–67. Paul was once again in Rome as a prisoner. But no longer was he staying in rented quarters, kept under house guard. Now he was held in the dungeon of the Mamartine Prison, chained like a common prisoner. This time, he received few visitors, and his friends had trouble finding him. As he wrote to his young friend Timothy, he knew that his life would soon come to an end. Tradition holds that Nero ordered Paul beheaded for his Christian faith.

Knowing what was ahead, Paul wrote words of encouragement to his younger coworker. Soon enough Timothy would be on his own, because Paul would soon be dead. As the persecution spread from Rome to other parts of the Empire, Paul feared that many Christians would crumble under the pressure. Even Timothy might not be able to stand. That's why this letter began on a very personal note. Paul reminded Timothy of his godly heritage handed down from his mother Eunice and his grandmother Lois (2 Timothy 1:5). He also recalled the moment of Timothy's ordination, when Timothy received "the gift of God" through the laying on of Paul's hands (v. 6). From that moment on, God had supernaturally endowed Timothy with whatever gifts he needed to fulfill his ministry.

It seems likely that Timothy's youth and the rising tide of opposition combined to produce a spirit of timidity. Such a problem might be normally overlooked. But in light of his approaching death, Paul dealt bluntly with it: "God didn't make you a coward." That spirit of fear didn't come from God, but from the adversary.

When God sends His Spirit, the result is always positive: power, love, and self-discipline. Power refers to the ability to accomplish things that the natural man or woman could never do. Love refers to the God-given ability to reach out in sympathetic compassion, even toward our enemies. Self-discipline speaks of the ability to focus our minds in the midst of many distractions.

Did Timothy need power? He already had it. Did he need love? He already had it. Did he need self-discipline? He already had it. These qualities always mark the person who lives under the control of the Holy Spirit.

Such words must have lifted Timothy and put the fire back in his soul. Too often Christians feel as though they need something "extra" from God —a second blessing, a crisis experience, a moment of emotional ecstasy. Those things may be good in themselves, but they do not constitute the key to the Christian life. We don't need anything "extra" from God. We simply need to appropriate what God has already given us.

No one needs to live in fear. No one needs to live with anger and bitterness. No one needs to live an unfocused life. God's Holy Spirit already indwells us. As soon as we tire of living by our own power, He will take over and produce in us those qualities we desperately seek.

When we need courage, love, or discipline, we should never say, "We can't," because in Christ, and through the Holy Spirit, God has said, "You can!"

Thank You, Father, for fully equipping me to face life. Show me the mighty resources that are mine through Your Holy Spirit. Amen.

He saved us through the washing of rebirth and renewal by the Holy Spirit, whom he poured out on us. (Titus 3:5)

A few years before Paul's death, Paul and Titus made a missionary visit to the island of Crete. After surveying the situation, Paul left Titus in Crete to provide leadership for the fledgling Christian church. Evidently Titus (a young man) became discouraged because of the deplorable condition in the local assemblies. Many were operating without qualified elders, leading to dysfunctional church life. Paul wrote to encourage his young lieutenant to stay in Crete, raise up godly elders, and provide solid teaching about proper relationships in the home, the church, and the workplace.

After some very practical, down-to-earth instruction, Paul balanced his message with the truth that the grace of God is the foundation of all Christian living. Those who understand God's grace have the ultimate motivation for godly living (2:11–14). Salvation by grace leads to gracious behavior toward those around us and in authority over us (2:15–3:2). Lest we forget, we were once lost in sin, but now have been given new life through Jesus Christ, which ought to result in truly changed behavior (3:3–8).

Two specific phrases in Titus 3:5 describe that new life: "The washing of rebirth," a reference to the removal of sin through the blood of Jesus Christ, and "renewal by the Holy Spirit," the imparting of new life. Thus the guilt of the past is completely removed and, in its place, the Holy Spirit brings about total inner renewal.

Note that the Holy Spirit is "poured out on us." This pictures more than the moment of initial salvation. God continually pours out the Holy Spirit on His children, ensuring that the new life will never grow old. This thought ought to be a great comfort to every struggling Christian. God wants us to have all the resources we need for the problems we face. That's why He poured out His Spirit—not a little trickle, but a mighty ocean from heaven.

Think about that. God washed all our sins away. He gave us brand-new lives. He also poured out the Holy Spirit upon us. He continually renews our hearts.

All that we need from God we already have. If we believe it and act upon it, we will discover that it is true.

Father, too often I focus on Your commandments as if You were a hard taskmaster. Remind me today that Your grace is sufficient for all my needs. Amen.

ETERNAL SPIRIT

How much more, then, will the blood of Christ, who through the eternal Spirit offered himself unblemished to God, cleanse our consciences from acts that lead to death, so that we may serve the living God! (Hebrews 9:14)

The first part of this verse contains a lovely reference to all three persons of the Godhead: Christ offered Himself (in His death) through the eternal Spirit to God. The phrase "eternal Spirit" occurs nowhere else in Scripture. It emphasizes that in His death—as in His life—Christ performed His mighty acts in the power of the Holy Spirit. As God, Christ could have worked His miracles in His own power. But as the perfect Man, He chose to rely upon the Spirit, thus providing a pattern for us to follow. When the moment came for Him to be offered as the "Lamb of God, who takes away the sin of the world" (John 1:29), He perfectly fulfilled the demands of the law by offering Himself "unblemished" by any moral stain or physical infirmity. His was a truly perfect sacrifice, thus acceptable to God. The writer of Hebrews tells us that in His death, Christ offered Himself to God through the "eternal Spirit." The word "eternal" stresses that though He died at a specific time in history, His death has eternal significance. Its effects are such that Christ can truly be called "the Lamb that was slain from the creation of the world" (Revelation 13:8).

Great consequences flow from such an awesome event. Hebrews 9:14 suggests two of them. First, we now have clean consciences, an enormous blessing to anyone who has ever known the power of guilt and shame. Second, we are now set free to serve the living God. While we were enslaved to sin, we could never please God. But through the death of Christ, those chains have been broken forever. Now we can serve God with confidence.

No wonder the New International Version ends this verse with an exclamation point. Reading it ought to fill us with joy. Christians, we've been set free. Rejoice. Sing. Laugh. Throw those chains away. Enjoy God. And serve with a smile.

Lord Jesus, it feels so good to finally be free. Words cannot express the joy I feel. Please accept my cheerful obedience as my way of saying, "Thank You." Amen.

The Spirit of grace. (Hebrews 10:29)

The book of Hebrews addressed genuine believers who, during a time of persecution, were sorely tempted to return to their Jewish roots. But if they had taken such a drastic step, they would have lost a great reward and ultimately faced the judgment of God. For them to leave the Christian church would have been the equivalent of deliberately sinning after receiving the knowledge of the truth (Hebrews 10:26). In that case, they would discover that there is no other sacrifice for sin. If you turn away from Jesus, you're leaving the only One who can forgive your sins. No one else can do what He does.

The only thing that is left for such a person is the expectation of God's judgment, a fact taught in the law of Moses (vv. 27–28). If God judged His people for the sin of unbelief in the Old Testament, the same sin will bring greater punishment during the age of grace (v. 29). The law itself reminds us of this truth (v. 30). It is a dreadful thing for a sinning believer to fall into God's hands for judgment (v. 31).

The particular sin envisioned has three parts: First, there is public rejection of Christ ("trampled the Son of God under foot"). Second, there is disrespect for the blood of Christ ("treated as an unholy thing the blood of the covenant that sanctified him"). Third, there is mocking the Holy Spirit ("insulted the Spirit of grace"). A person committing such a sin deserves God's harsh punishment.

Could a genuine believer ever do such a thing? The answer seems to be yes. In fact, it seems likely that only a believer could sin this way. More than that, this sin (however rare it may be) can only be committed by those who have been Christians for a fairly long period of time. Of all people, they should know better because they have experienced the riches of God's salvation. On the other hand, an unbeliever has never been truly "sanctified" by the blood of Christ.

In that light, the title "Spirit of grace" comes into clear focus. Only willful, presumptuous, hard-hearted believers who rebel in the face of all that God's Spirit has done for them can commit such a sin.

Such a prospect ought to fill every believer with godly fear. When Jesus announced that one of the disciples would betray Him, they individually (and rightly) replied, "Lord, is it I?" (Matthew 26:22 KJV). Peter boasted that he would never deny His Lord, but he fell into sin less than four hours later.

God's grace ought to lead us to righteous living, but our self-confidence may lead us into unexpected sin. Take nothing for granted. Guard your heart. Keep short accounts with God.

If we follow Jesus with grateful hearts, we have nothing to fear.

Keep me true to You, Lord Jesus, lest I should begin to drift away. May I never take You for granted, not even for a moment. Amen.

HOLY SPIRIT SENT FROM HEAVEN

Those who have preached the Gospel to you by the Holy Spirit sent from heaven. (1 Peter 1:12)

How much did the Old Testament prophets understand about the coming of Christ? Much, but not everything. They knew, for instance, that the Messiah would be born at Bethlehem (Micah 5:2), to a virgin (Isaiah 7:14), that He would come from the line of David (Isaiah 11:1–3), that He would be rejected by His people (Isaiah 53:1–3), that He would someday reign over Israel and the nations of the earth (Psalm 2; 110; Zechariah 14). Many other details were revealed in isolated bits and pieces. What the prophets lacked was a big picture view of the Messiah's coming to the earth. Specifically, they never understood that the Messiah would come twice to the earth, once as a babe in the manger and once to rule as king from David's throne in Jerusalem. They saw the two comings of Christ as one sees two mountain peaks in the distance, without perceiving the valley between them.

When Peter wrote to encourage Christians who were suffering for their faith, he reminded his readers that their salvation was prophesied in the Old Testament. However, the prophets did not always understand their own words. For that reason, they "searched intently and with the greatest care" (1 Peter 1:10), studying the minute details of what God revealed, trying to understand what it all meant. In those days the Spirit of Christ spoke through them with many detailed predictions concerning the Messiah's coming, suffering, and future glory. None of them knew the whole story or saw the entire picture of God's plan. Isaiah saw a part, Jeremiah saw a part, and Daniel saw a part. But no one saw it all or understood it all. In that sense, the prophets of old were serving not themselves (or even their own generation exclusively) but future generations of believers who would understand the prophecies after they had been fulfilled.

How is it that we today know more than Isaiah or Jeremiah or Daniel? Only because someone came and preached the Gospel to us "by the Holy Spirit sent from heaven." Left to ourselves, we would never understand God's plan on our own. Illumination comes to the human heart through the preaching of the Word of God in the power of the Holy Spirit.

This ministry of the Spirit is often unappreciated. He takes the words that are preached and causes them to penetrate the human heart. He gives "fresh oil" to the preacher so that his words go deep within us. In the parable of the sower (Matthew 13:1–23), some seed fell on the road, some on rocky soil, some among thorns, and some on the good soil where it brought forth good fruit. What makes the difference? Surely it is the condition of the human heart. But the heart becomes "good soil" only through the divine intervention of the "Holy Spirit sent from heaven."

The phrase "sent from heaven" doubtless refers to the day of Pentecost, when the ascended Christ poured out the Holy Spirit (Acts 2), resulting in miracles and the conversion of three thousand people. That same Holy Spirit animates the preaching of the Gospel and makes it effective in human hearts today.

Holy Spirit, thank You for faithful pastors and Bible teachers. Fill them with power as they preach and teach. Give me ears to hear what You are saying and a willing heart to respond in obedience. Amen.

If you are insulted because of the name of Christ, you are blessed, for the Spirit of glory and of God rests on you. (1 Peter 4:14)

Suffering is the universal experience of all faithful Christians. Jesus said as much to His disciples in the Sermon on the Mount: "Blessed are you when people insult you, persecute you and falsely say all kinds of evil against you because of Me. Rejoice and be glad" (Matthew 5:11–12). Following Jesus means taking up the cross of suffering, shame and rejection by the world. That theme is amplified in 1 Peter 4:12–19, showing how suffering and the will of God go together. How should we respond when suffering comes? First, we need not be surprised (v. 12). Second, we are to rejoice (v. 13). Third, we can realize that the "Spirit of glory" rests on us (v. 14). Fourth, we need to make sure we aren't suffering because of our own sins (v. 15). Fifth, we can praise God for the privilege of bearing His name (v. 16). Sixth, we must understand that judgment always begins with God's people first (vv. 17–18). Seventh, we can commit ourselves to God and continue to do good (v. 19).

Again and again, Peter mentioned the present blessing and the future reward for believers who patiently suffer for their faith. Though things may be hard now, we will one day be overjoyed as we share in the reward God has for faithful saints. But even in the present difficulties, there are many compensations. Suffering believers experience God's faithfulness, they share intimately in Christ's sufferings, they have the high privilege of bearing the name of God in the world, they have the consolation of knowing that other believers are suffering with them, and the "Spirit of glory" rests on them.

This particular title—Spirit of glory—is very meaningful because glory is one of God's fundamental attributes. In Acts 7:2, Luke calls Him the "God of glory." Jesus reveals to us the glory of God (John 1:17). In the Old Testament, God's glory revealed the splendor of God's presence with His people. To see God's glory was to see God Himself—as much as any person could ever see of God. By means of the Holy Spirit's indwelling, the God of glory has come to live within us. We have a privilege that the saints of old never knew —the permanent dwelling of God in our hearts.

Anything we suffer for Christ is a blessing, not a burden because the Holy Spirit makes the suffering worthwhile. Just as the angels ministered to Christ after His temptation, even so God will minister to us through the Holy Spirit when we are tempted to despair and give up our faith.

God never takes lightly the suffering of His children. As we endure hard times with patient cheerfulness, the "Spirit of glory" enables us to handle whatever happens with grace and dignity.

This may not make suffering easy or enjoyable, but it does put it in a positive light. We know that our hard times are never wasted, but are used by God for our good and His glory.

Suffering for Christ brings a deeper experience of the Holy Spirit today—and a great reward tomorrow.

But we have to go through the hard times first. The glory comes later.

Spirit of glory, fill me with courage so that I may endure hardship without complaining. Make me like Jesus even if that means sharing in His suffering. Amen.

THE ANOINTING

As for you, the anointing you received from him remains in you, and you do not need anyone to teach you. (1 John 2:27)

This verse has occasionally given rise to some strange interpretations. Some have suggested that since all believers have "the anointing," they don't need human teachers. Unfortunately, people who say such things are themselves the best refutation of that interpretation.

Whatever else 1 John 2:27 means, it can't be intended to disparage human teachers, since Ephesians 4:11–13 clearly indicates that the ascended Christ gives Spirit-filled teachers as one of His gifts to the church. Romans 12:7 also tells us that if a person's gift is teaching, let him or her teach. Why give the gift of teaching if human teachers aren't needed?

The background of 1 John helps us understand this verse. Evidently a loose collection of false teachers had gained a foothold among the Christian churches of Asia Minor (modern-day Turkey). These "antichrists" (John's word for them) denied the Incarnation of Christ, downplayed the importance of obeying God's commands, and implied that secret knowledge is given to a few people (themselves) who must be blindly followed.

It is the latter false teaching which John confronted in 1 John 2:27. The issue is not whether we should receive instruction from others. Certainly all Christians can benefit from the ministry of Spirit-directed teachers. It edifies the saints and builds up the body of Christ. Solid teaching produces mature believers. Without good teachers, the church loses its spiritual vigor and may become prey to being tossed about by any wind of strange doctrine.

The question behind 1 John 2:27 might be phrased something like this: Am I required to be dependent on particular human teachers for my spiritual growth? The false teachers had evidently led many believers into an unhealthy dependence on their unique (and heretical) teaching. Doubtless, they couched their words in pet phraseology and proclaimed their allegiance to the true apostles. But like all cult leaders, their teaching produced the exaltation of man, not God.

Against such an unhealthy dependence, John taught his readers that because they had received the "anointing" of the Holy Spirit, they are no longer obliged to go to another person (or group of people) in order to be right with God or to understand God's Word. In this sense, 1 John 2:27 is a corollary to the Reformation doctrines of the priesthood of the believer and the perspicuity of Scripture. Those two doctrines teach that believers are free to go directly to God, without going through any human intermediaries (such as priests or authoritative teachers). What John added to those two truths is the vital reason those doctrines are true:

The "anointing" of the Spirit (which is really another word for the indwelling of the Spirit) enables even the simplest believer to understand the message of salvation for himself or herself—with or without the aid of human teachers.

God made it simple so that all of us could be saved. He made the Gospel clear so that anyone with an open mind and an open heart can understand it. And He gave each Christian the "anointing" of the Spirit to enable us to read the Bible and discover its truth on our own.

Does this do away with the need for teachers? By no means. In fact, it encourages good teaching because it means that hearers have the spiritual power to absorb what is being said. In short, they have the power to think for themselves.

The best teachers depend upon the Holy Spirit in two ways: (1) once to help the teacher, and (2) once again to help the hearers. Thus the whole learning process is dependent not on humans, but on God whose Word is being taught.

Holy Spirit, bless all those who teach Your Word. Grant them great power, and grant discernment and wisdom for those who listen. Amen.

We know it by the Spirit he gave us.
(1 John 3:24)

The perceptive reader cannot help but notice how many times the Bible writers return to the theme of the indwelling of the Holy Spirit. This verse ties the believer's outward obedience to God to the reality of the Spirit dwelling within, thus providing a twofold check on our Christian life: (1) Are we daily obeying God's commands? (2) Are we living in harmony with the Holy Spirit?

Neither question is the slightest bit mystical. In 1 John, obeying God's commands comes down to practical things like loving our brother instead of hating him. John likes to think in dualities. We can't love the invisible God while at the same time hating our very visible brother.

In 1 John 4, we learn that living in harmony with the Spirit involves testing the "spirits" to see what they say about Jesus Christ. If they do not acknowledge that Jesus has come in the flesh, they are not of God. This may seem arcane to some of us, but it is perfectly in line with the fact that the Holy Spirit glorifies the Son.

Here, then, is a good daily test for our spiritual lives. First, what have we done in the last twenty-four hours that has shown our love (or lack thereof) for our Christian brothers and sisters? It doesn't have to be big or flashy, but there ought to be some answer. Second, what have we done in the last twenty-four hours that brought glory (in one way or another) to Jesus Christ? Most of us may stumble over that question, but our stumbling reveals something about how easy it is to become self-centered Christians.

Try this test for seven days. It might change your life. It will certainly improve it.

Lord, save me from the temptation to talk the talk without walking the walk. Make me a real Christian, not a cheap imitation. Amen.

GOD'S TESTIMONY

We accept man's testimony, but God's testimony is greater. (1 John 5:9)

How do we know that the Christian faith is true? How can we be sure that Jesus Christ is the Son of God? What evidence is there that Jesus really is the only way to God?

Many unbelievers (and some Christians) struggle with these questions. After all, we live in a religious marketplace where Christianity is often seen as "just another religion" alongside Buddhism, Islam, Judaism, and New Age mysticism. The result for many secular people is often a religious smorgasbord, a little of this and a little of that. Not long ago a friend of mine mentioned an eminent surgeon who likes to boast of his cosmopolitan tastes in music and the arts. What is his religious background? "Oh, he embraces them all," my friend said, meaning it not as a compliment but simply as an observation.

Too many people "embrace them all," hoping that in the end God (if there is a God) will smile indulgently and let them into heaven.

In sharp contrast to such befuddled thinking we have the simple, majestic words of the apostle John: "He who has the Son has life; he who does not have the Son of God does not have life" (1 John 5:12). These words are simple, clear, and utterly exclusive. When it comes to salvation, there are only two options: We either have the Son or we don't. There is no choice for those who want to "embrace them all."

When John spoke of "God's testimony," he was really referring to the objective truth about Jesus Christ, centering on His life, death, burial, and resurrection. These are sober facts of history, not flights of religious fancy. God's testimony is wrapped up not in a doctrine, but in a person— Jesus Christ. The truth God wants us to know is really the Truth with a capital "T." Christianity is not a religion at all, but a relationship with God's Son.

Those who enter into that relationship have God's testimony in another sense—the Holy Spirit living within. That's what John meant by the phrase "this testimony in his heart" (v. 10). It is the Holy Spirit who takes the objective reality of Christ and makes it real in the human heart. *The Living Bible* translates it this way: "All who believe this know in their hearts it is true" (v. 10).

How, then, can we know that the Christian faith is true? First, because it rests on the bedrock truth of the life, death, and resurrection of Jesus Christ. Second, because the Holy Spirit has taken this bedrock truth and made it real in our hearts. In the same way, we know that Jesus is the only way to heaven because God has said so, and because the Holy Spirit has made that truth real in our hearts.

The objective truth always comes first. Our faith rests upon the facts of history. But without God's testimony in our hearts, we would still never believe it.

We may be sure of our faith because God has said it, and because His Spirit has also enabled us to believe it.

Sovereign Lord, Your Word is truth and Your Spirit is life. Thank You for giving me both so that I may share my faith with confidence. Amen.

SEVEN SPIRITS OF GOD

These are the seven spirits of God.
(Revelation 4:5)

Four times the Book of Revelation refers to the "seven spirits" of God (1:4, 3:1, 4:5, 5:6). This unusual phrase occurs nowhere else in Scripture. Many commentators connect it with the sevenfold Spirit of God mentioned in Isaiah 11:1–2 and the lampstand with seven lights in Zechariah 4:2. The number "7" in Scripture (and especially in Revelation) often denotes completeness or perfection. Thus, the seven seals, seven trumpets, and seven bowls (all mentioned in Revelation) speak of the completeness of God's judgment on the earth.

In Revelation 1:4, the "seven spirits" are seen before the throne of God. In Revelation 3:1, Christ is seen holding the "seven spirits" along with the "seven stars"—the messengers (angelic or human) of the seven churches. In Revelation 4:5, the "seven spirits" are the seven lamps blazing before the throne (a clear allusion to Zechariah 4). In Revelation 5:6, the "seven spirits" are the seven eyes of the Lamb (Christ).

Each reference adds a bit to our knowledge of the Holy Spirit and His work. In Revelation 1:4 we are told that the Holy Spirit is truly part of the Trinity (He is mentioned after the Father and before the Son). Revelation 3:1 shows us that the Holy Spirit serves the Son by empowering His body, the church. Revelation 4:5 adds the fact that the Holy

Spirit is the light of heaven, and Revelation 5:6 shows that the Holy Spirit serves as the "eyes of Christ" on the earth.

All of this may seem strange to us, but it made perfect sense to the first-century readers who were steeped in biblical symbolism. The Holy Spirit is called the "seven spirits of God" to show the completeness both of His person and of His ministry. He is always part of the Trinity, always before the throne, and always serving and glorifying the Son. He is the divine power that enables the church to be a shining light in a darkened world.

This truth should bring great encouragement to God's servants who often serve in difficult situations. Let us always remember that it is "not by might nor by power, but by my Spirit," (Zechariah 4:6) that God's work goes forward. His Spirit is the power source that gives believers strength to face persecution (as in Smyrna), that raises a dead church back to life (as in Sardis), that opens doors for ministry (as in Philadelphia). When we are tempted to give up because the going is rough, we must remember that God's Spirit is always there, going before us, creating a way through the impossible.

Gracious Father, Your Spirit enables me to do more than I think I can. Keep me in touch with Your Spirit especially when I am tempted to quit too soon. Amen.

SPIRIT OF PROPHECY

For the testimony of Jesus is the spirit of prophecy. (Revelation 19:10)

The final title of the Holy Spirit comes from a strange (and often-overlooked) passage in Revelation 19. The apostle John was overwhelmed by the vision of the second coming of Christ to the earth. He saw the destruction of Babylon, heard the sound of the choirs of heaven singing together in praise to God, heard the voice of God coming from the throne, watched as the elders and the living creatures fell down and worshiped God.

Sound. Thunder. Shouting. Roars of rushing water.

"Hallelujah! For our Lord God Almighty reigns" (v. 6)

At that moment, an angel spoke to John, telling him to write a blessing for those invited to the wedding supper of the Lamb. It was simply too much for the apostle, who fell to his feet and began to worship the angel. The angel stopped him by saying, "I am a fellow servant with you and with your brothers who hold to the testimony of Jesus. Worship God!" (Revelation 19:10).

The "testimony of Jesus" is the truth about who He is, why He came, and what He accomplished in His death and resurrection. These things are the "spirit of prophecy." The words of true prophets come directly from the Holy Spirit. He inspires and fills them with the truth of Christ, which they then share with others.

We close this study of the Holy Spirit by returning once again to His central ministry of bringing glory to Jesus Christ. Today, one of the special functions of the Spirit is to point believers to Jesus by making Christ real to them. All the Bible points to Him. History is truly His Story. He is the most important person in the universe, the central figure of the human race, and the Savior of the world.

Does it seem unlikely to end a book about the Holy Spirit by talking about Jesus? It shouldn't, because the Spirit Himself came to point us toward the Son of God. My prayer is that Holy Spirit will fill each of us with His presence so that we will know and love Jesus Christ as never before. If that happens, the Father will be pleased, the Son glorified, and the Spirit satisfied.

Spirit of God, I have learned Your many titles and have been amazed at Your many unseen ministries. May this knowledge lead me to deeper devotion to Jesus, whom You came to glorify. Amen.

INDEX

Anointing (1 John 2:27), 199

Breath of the Almighty (Job 32:8; 33:4; 34:14–15), 29
Breath of Life (Genesis 2:7), 13
Breath of the Lord (Isaiah 40:7), 53

Circumcision (Romans 2:29), 125
Clothing (Luke 24:49), 92
Counselor (John 14:16), 102

Deposit (Ephesians 1:14), 168
Dew (Hosea 14:5), 69
Double Portion (2 Kings 2:9, 15), 21
Dove (Matthew 3:16), 79

Eternal Spirit (Hebrews 9:14), 189
Eyes of the Lord (Zechariah 4:10), 73

Finger of God (Luke 11:20), 90
Fire (Acts 2:3), 110
Firstfruits (Romans 8:23), 136

Gift (Acts 2:38), 115
God (Acts 5:3–4), 118
God's Testimony (1 John 5:9), 204

Hand of God (2 Chronicles 30:12), 23

His Holy Spirit (Isaiah 63:10–11), 63
His Spirit (Isaiah 48:16), 59
Holy Spirit Sent From Heaven (1 Peter 1:12), 193
Holy Spirit of God (Ephesians 4:30), 173
Holy Spirit Who Is In You (1 Corinthians 6:19), 147
Holy Spirit Whom He Poured Out (Titus 3:5), 187

Lamp of the Lord (Proverbs 20:27), 38
Lord Who Is the Spirit (2 Corinthians 3:18), 158

Mind of the Lord (Isaiah 40:13), 55
My Spirit (Genesis 6:3), 14

New Spirit (Ezekiel 11:19), 67

Oil (1 Samuel 16:13), 19
One Spirit (1 Corinthians 12:13), 153

Power of the Lord (Luke 5:17), 88
Power of the Most High (Luke 1:35), 85
Promise (Galatians 3:14), 160
Promised Holy Spirit (Acts 2:33), 112

Same Spirit (1 Corinthians 12:4), 150
Seal (Ephesians 1:13), 165
Servant (Genesis 24:34), 16

Seven Spirits of God (Revelation 4:5), 207

Spirit, The (Matthew 12:31), 83

Spirit Above the Waters (Genesis 1:2), 11

Spirit From On High (Isaiah 32:15), 51

Spirit Given Without Limit (John 3:34), 97

Spirit He Gave Us (1 John 3:24), 202

Spirit Himself (Romans 8:26), 138

Spirit of Christ (Romans 8:9), 129

Spirit of Counsel and Power (Isaiah 11:2), 45

Spirit of Glory (1 Peter 4:14), 196

Spirit of God (Genesis 41:38), 18

Spirit of Grace (Hebrews 10:29), 191

Spirit of Grace and Supplication (Zechariah
12:10), 75

Spirit of Him Who Raised Jesus from the
Dead (Romans 8:11), 131

Spirit of His Son (Galatians 4:6), 162

Spirit of Holiness (Romans 1:4), 123

Spirit of Jesus (Acts 16:7), 120

Spirit of Jesus Christ (Philippians 1:19), 179

Spirit of Judgment and Fire (Isaiah 4:4), 40

Spirit of Justice (Isaiah 28:6), 49

Spirit of Knowledge and of the Fear of the
Lord (Isaiah 11:2), 46

Spirit of Life in Christ Jesus (Romans 8:2),
127

Spirit of the Living God (2 Corinthians 3:3),
155

Spirit of the Lord (Micah 2:7), 71

Spirit of Our God (1 Corinthians 6:11), 144

Spirit of Power, Love and Self-Discipline
    (2 Timothy 1:7), 184
Spirit of Prophecy (Revelation 19:10), 209
Spirit of Sonship (Romans 8:15), 133
Spirit of the Sovereign Lord (Isaiah 61:1), 61
Spirit of Truth (John 14:17), 105
Spirit of Your Father (Matthew 10:20), 81
Spirit of Wisdom and Understanding (Isaiah
    11:2), 42
Spirit of Wisdom and Revelation (Ephesians
    1:17), 170
Spirit Who Gives Rest (Isaiah 63:14), 65
Spirit Who Goes Out From the Father (John
    15:26), 108
Spirit Who Is From God (1 Corinthians 2:12),
    141
Streams of Living Water (John 7:38), 100
Streams on the Dry Ground (Isaiah 44:3), 57

Vindicator of Christ (1 Timothy 3:16), 182

Water (Zechariah 14:8), 77
Wind (John 3:8), 95
Wine (Ephesians 5:18), 176

Your Good Spirit (Nehemiah 9:20), 25
Your Holy Spirit (Psalm 51:11), 31
Your Presence (Psalm 139:7), 36
Your Spirit (Nehemiah 9:30), 27
Your Spirit of Creation and Renewal (Psalm
    104:30), 34